# thrive

## How to Do Well in ANY Economy

CHUCK BENTLEY

D0957168

Portions of this book taken from content previously published in *The Root of Riches* and in *The S.A.L.T. Plan*™, also by Chuck Bentley.

November 2012 Edition

# Dedication

This book is dedicated to my friend and brother in Christ, Joe Coney, who knows how to thrive in any economy.

In 2012, Joe was honored by the Board of Directors of Crown Financial Ministries with the *Larry Burkett Servant Leadership Award* for his outstanding example of service in the advancement of God's financial principles. Joe's life continues to impact countless people around the world.

# contents

# foreword

The world has seen major economic turbulence in the past one hundred years, and I'm not just referring to America's Great Depression. Germany, Argentina, Zimbabwe and Iceland have all experienced a near total collapse of their banks or their currency, driven by a combination of factors that were slightly different in each case. It can happen to any nation, rich or poor. And it can happen on a personal level, even when the national economy is strong.

Iceland, a nation of only 320,000 people, ranks near the top of the list for quality of life and per capita income when measured against the rest of the world. In spite of this incredible abundance today, in 2008, the country's banking system imploded. Speculative lending practices by the nation's three largest banks generated massive financial losses too big for the government to cover with a bailout. In fact, relative to the size of its economy, this banking collapse ranks as the largest suffered by any nation in history. The ISK or króna lost over 60 percent of its value at one point. While not as devastating as the hyperinflation seen in other nations like Zimbabwe, this shock to Iceland's currency valuation was a painful fall for a people who prize their self-sufficiency.

My friend, Bjorg (not his real name, but it does mean "protection") from Iceland attended a Crown conference in 2010, some time after his nation's economic meltdown occurred. It was great to hear how he had been living by God's financial principles before, during and after the banking collapse. He gave testimony that it had little effect on him or his family. I was so encouraged by his report that I asked to meet with him privately to hear more about how he managed to avoid the fate of most of his countrymen.

He explained that the primary problem was one of greed. Demand for the króna had been increasing steadily on the world market, making it more valuable against other currencies. To take full advantage of this benefit, locals were mortgaging their homes in a weaker currency than the króna. This method, although risky, captured the attention of most of his countrymen and they began buying or building bigger homes—homes they never could have afforded without this currency advantage.

Bjorg knew that the Bible warned against greed, excessive debt and risky ventures. Not only did he refuse to get caught up in the spirit of materialism and overspending, he tried to warn his friends. Few would listen and most considered him foolish for missing out on this seemingly fantastic opportunity to upgrade his lifestyle. In spite of the pressures, he refused.

When the bubble finally burst, the króna fell quickly against the currencies used to finance the risky home mortgages. The trend was now going the other direction and many of those mortgage holders were quickly underwater. By being debt free, avoiding any new debt and being diversified in his investments, Bjorg lost only a portion of his net worth when the economic tsunami hit, while others—including many of his friends and family—lost their homes and experienced painful financial setbacks. And while others were still rebuilding, Bjorg was able to prosper—giving, saving, and investing just as before. In the end, he could look back and see how yielding his life to God and His financial principles gave him the confident foundation he needed to make wise decisions while those around him were taken in by a foolish venture.

The purpose of this book is to help you be a "Bjorg" right where you live—to know God's financial principles and apply them, regardless of the economic challenges you may face. Actually, that's only part of what we hope these principles will do for you. Applying God's principles to your life has the power, not only to help you survive, but to thrive!

We at Crown are here to help you do just that, so please visit *crown.org* to learn more.

Chuck Bentley
CEO, Crown Financial Ministries
Lawrenceville, Georgia
November 1, 2012

thrive | **chapter 1**

# Stormproof Your Finances

I have a close friend who manages his family's business, which he took over from his father. In the early 1980s, he became very concerned about the global economic slowdown. The business was experiencing extreme stress at the time, as sales had slowed to a crawl. My friend's father had founded the company more than 40 years earlier, and had weathered the ups and downs of many economic storms. He was considered very wise by all those who knew him. And so, feeling the weight of the world on his shoulders, my friend made an appointment to sit down with his now seventy-year-old father, looking for some comforting words and counsel.

When they met, he asked a slew of questions, seeking to gain a better understanding of the global economy, and hoping he might use that information to develop a plan for navigating the complex problems his family's company faced.

His father simply said, "The economy goes up, and the economy goes down. Remember this and plan accordingly." That was all he said. And that was enough. My friend was stunned by the simplicity of his father's advice. But fortunately for his siblings who depended on him to lead the company through the crisis, he never forgot that fundamental principle. As a result, the company continues to be strong long after his father's death.

Warren Buffett once said, "It's only when the tide goes out that you learn who's been swimming naked." For some, a dramatic change in financial circumstances can be not only embarrassing, but also revealing. Far too many Americans live blissfully but foolishly unprepared for the inevitable sudden changes in the economy.

The reality is that the strongest economy in the world has seen sixteen recessions since 1932. The unpredictable ups and downs of the economy are the constant. The real variable is whether or not we are prepared.

We should consider the words of Jesus in this parable as His commentary on global economic challenges:

> "Everyone then who hears these words of mine and does them will be like a wise man who built his house on the rock. And the rain fell, and the floods came, and the winds blew and beat on that house, but it did not fall, because it had been founded on the rock. And everyone who hears these words of mine and does not do them will be like a foolish man who built his house on the sand. And the rain fell, and the floods came, and the winds blew and beat against that house, and it fell, and great was the fall of it" (MATTHEW 7:24-27).

This parable illustrates that storms are not optional. The Christian and non-Christian are both battered by the same storms, trials and tests. One, however, is prepared for stormy weather—the one who has *acted upon* God's Truth.

In the last few years, we've witnessed the world shifting like sand beneath our feet. We've been asking ourselves, "What's happened to us?" "Is it ever going back to the way it used to be?" "What kind of adjustments do we need to make to prepare for the future?"

People all around the world are experiencing a new level of insecurity. The things they placed their hope and confidence in have disappointed them. There is now a sense of fear, restlessness, and anxiety lingering just beneath the surface.

> We are in the midst of an economic storm today, and every Christian must decide whether to build upon the solid rock of God's Word or the shifting sands of society.

You may be asking yourself, "Where is the leader who's going to show us the way out of this?" "Are we ever going back to the day when we had rising home equity values?" "Are we ever going back to the day when we could put our money into institutions or companies and trust them to operate with integrity?" "Will there be a time when the banks will not fail, when my job may not be going away or my hours cut back?" "Can I go to college, get a degree, and know that I'll have a secure career path for the rest of my life?"

The Lord told us that a house (or life) built upon sand will fall when storms come, but one built upon the Rock will survive. We are in the midst of an economic storm today, and every Christian must decide whether to build upon the solid rock of God's Word or the shifting sands of society. If our decisions are guided by the world's normal standards (guile and deception), we are inadvertently making decisions to deny Christ. *"No servant can serve two masters, for either he will hate the one and love the other, or he will be devoted to the one and despise the other. You cannot serve God and money"* (Luke16:13).

Each Christian must learn to recognize that God's approval is more important than the world's riches. Then, and only then, will the full measure of God's peace and power be experienced. The world will tell you that your purposes, goals, significance, self-worth, ambition and life energy should be wrapped up in having money: Make as much as you can, as quickly as you can, to retire as soon as you can, and enjoy a life of leisure and security as long as you can is the not so subtle philosophy of millions of people trapped in a life working only so that one day they can go on a long vacation.

You've been told that if you have enough money, you can live free of fear and anxiety—comfortably insulated from what's going on around you. If you focus on the things of this world, you'll place your hope in your net worth, in your assets, and in your ability to generate income. In short, money will become your master.

But by focusing on God and His promises, you can be prepared for the future no matter what it may be. You now have the opportunity, by God's grace, to reset your thinking, to be transformed, not conformed to the world (Romans 12:2).

Learning to view money God's way begins with understanding that His economy is made up of the divine integration of His lordship, your stewardship and your generosity.

When those elements come together, you are transformed by the renewing of your mind. Steadily, you'll be freed from the cultural pressure and grip of this world, and you'll experience victory in the battle that wants to take you captive.

When God is Lord, He is the object of your life. The Bible says in Matthew 6:33 to seek first His kingdom and His righteousness, so use your energy to seek His kingdom first, rather than merely pursuing your own needs and wants. In God's kingdom, He is recognized as Lord of all, and our charge is to seek to please Him above all else.

The world will always be changing and unstable, but God is constant. As such, we can trust Him and have contentment regardless of our circumstances. Hebrews 13:5 tells us, *"Keep your lives free from the love of money* [in other words, keep your life free from buying into the lies of the world] *and be content with what you have [whether a lot or a little]"* (NIV).

When you are content with what you have, you can rest in the promise found in the remainder of that verse: *"Never will I leave you; never will I forsake you."* The Lord is telling you that when you fix your gaze on the things of this world, you are vulnerable; everything can leave and forsake you, except for Him.

In our world, success is defined by how much you have, and how much you can accumulate. But when you understand

God's lordship, your will begin to define success by whether or not you are faithful with what you have.

Success in God's eyes has nothing to do with how much you can accumulate. In His economy, if you are faithful with little, you will be entrusted with much. You will be entrusted with "true riches" (Luke 16:11).

God defines success as the faithful management of whatever you have been given, whether much or little. When God is the first priority and the object of your life, your desire will be the responsible stewardship of whatever you have, and you will strive to be generous in every circumstance. You will start to believe and practice the principle that it is better to give than to receive (Acts 20:35).

For many people today, it is better to receive, hoard, and have a big line of credit. These are all things the world says are required to have success and significance. But God says it is better to be a giver.

When you understand what the Bible says about money and are transformed by what you believe, your behavior will follow suit as you submit to God's lordship. Applying the practical truths of handling money God's way, you will then experience the visible joy of living in step with His Spirit distinct from the rest of the world.

This distinction becomes your visual testimony, demonstrating the difference between having God integrated into all of your finances and trusting in yourself only. You will display joy on your face and peace in your heart while everyone else is wondering, "Where is our hope?" The fleeting hopes of this world will transfer into the eternal hope of Christ.

Are you different from your next-door neighbor in what you believe about money, how you steward it and how generous you are? Have your neighbors witnessed the difference in you? Understanding that God is good and that He's in control of circumstances keeps you from being trapped, worried and grieving over something very temporal. Your joy becomes the attractive aroma of Christ.

Christ is unchanging; His principles work. They are valid and time tested, and they hold up in every storm. You and I have the privilege of sharing that with the world. It can change our neighborhoods, our cities, our nation, and the entire world if we apply the truth, model it and live it out.

I encourage you to move away from defining your life by the standards of this world and to become an ambassador for Christ in this generation. Your transformation will help bring about the revival that our nation desperately needs, regardless of the circumstances you may face.

## Trajectory Makes All the Difference

Our late co-founder Larry Burkett did not become a follower of Jesus Christ until he was an adult. At the time, he was working as a contractor for the NASA space program. But he left that behind to eventually launch a ministry called Christian Financial Concepts (which later became Crown), believing that sharing biblical truth about our finances was more important than putting more men on the moon.

When Larry experienced the joy of his new birth, he realized that he knew very little about the Bible or Christianity, having not been raised in the faith. This void led him to pray a very sincere prayer: "Lord, You know I don't know much about You or Your Word, so You will have to be tolerant of my ignorance; but You will never have to be concerned with my obedience. Please reveal more and more of Your truth to me and I will gladly obey You." With that heart attitude, Larry applied himself to the study of God's Word, soaking up every new principle he learned, including financial principles.

> **How might God use you if you commit your life and your finances to Him in obedience to His Word?**

From that simple commitment, Larry was used by God to touch millions of lives around the world. How might God use you if you commit your life and your finances to Him in obedience to His Word?

# Discover God's Design for Work

Contrary to popular opinion, charity is not God's solution to poverty. Work is. Yes, there are times when God does provide through the kindness of others, and God is able to provide for us in the most extreme of circumstances. Remember that Elijah was fed by ravens delivering him food. Now that's a special delivery! But the normal means of God's daily provision is our profitable work. That's why, among other reasons, He wants us to work hard wherever we find ourselves and regardless of the economic forecast.

> "Work gives meaning to life . . . Work
> is the form in which we make ourselves
> useful to others." [1]

This quote, by Lester DeKoster, the former director of the Calvin College and Seminary library, condenses the importance of this simple yet profound truth, that work is the basis for all that we are put on earth to accomplish.

For many, the word *work* has so many negative associations that they'd just as soon skip the discussion altogether. One of the great tragedies of our day is the great number of people who, in survey after survey, indicate dissatisfaction with their jobs. But work was not intended to be drudgery.

In the beginning, before sin even entered the picture, the Bible tells us, *"The LORD God took the man and put him in the Garden of Eden to work it and keep it"* (GENESIS 2:15). Work was not an afterthought or a necessary evil that came into being after the Fall. Rather, it was an essential part of God's design for human beings from the start.

Something did change after our first parents sinned though, which explains the frustration many people associate with their work. To Adam, God said, *"Cursed is the ground because of you; in pain you shall eat of it all the days of your life; thorns and thistles it shall bring forth for you; and you shall eat the plants of the field. By the sweat of your face you shall eat bread"* (GENESIS 3:17-19). Your job may not put you in direct contact with thorns and thistles every day, but the difficulties associated with working in our fallen world are all too real.

Work is one of the primary ways we experience purpose, meaning and joy. It's what we were created to do…work and *produce*. In fact, not working takes a greater toll on us in the long run. I'm not suggesting that we shouldn't rest or take care of our bodies, but avoiding work *altogether* is the road to misery and ruin. Such a lifestyle is contrary to our very design.

Chuck Colson, the late founder of Prison Fellowship, once said, *"God created human beings in His own image and part of being 'in His image' means that we are workers— like God Himself. That's where that innate, inner drive for work comes from. Work is part of God's nature."* [2]

Since we are created in God's image and divinely ordained for work, we are to rule over the earth as caretakers and managers on God's behalf. This distinctive trait allows for self-expression, the potential to be used for great causes to serve the needs of the world and to bring glory to God in the process.

As followers of Christ, our work should be excellent in every way. Christians should be the most desired of all employees or employers in the world. Why? Because we believe in the dignity of hard work and strive to do our best with the motivation that we are representing the God who created us for His purposes. His Word gives us clear instruction to work hard:

> *"Whatever your hands find to do, do it with your might"* (ECCLESIASTES 9:10).

> *"Six days you shall work"* (EXODUS 34:21).

> *"If anyone is not willing to work, let him not eat."* (2 THESSALONIANS 3:10).

In my travels, I've experienced cultures where work is not valued or practiced among the men in the community. The consequences that result from these practices are always misery, suffering and extreme poverty. Far too often, Christians attempt to treat only the symptoms of poverty through generosity and charitable help alone. Unfortunately, if we avoid dealing with the root issue in these cultures, a lack of knowledge of God and His teachings, their errant beliefs remain unchanged. Misery simply returns when the giving stops.

> **Christians should be the most desired of all employees or employers in the world.**

However, if we make it our mission to instill the values of stewardship and accountability in this community, the bountiful fruit produced by transformed people will be an ongoing witness to the goodness of God and His ways. But that's not all!

Lester DeKoster expanded his insight into the exponential impact of our work on the whole of civilization:

> *"Lay a blanket of seeds upon a field, and behold, a harvest! Lay a blanket of work upon the world, and behold, a civilization!"* [3]

# Work to Take Care of Your Family

*"But if anyone does not provide for his relatives, and especially for members of his household, he has denied the faith and is worse than an unbeliever"* (1 Timothy 5:8).

God's financial plan is balanced. He has given us the primary responsibility of caring for our own flesh and blood. While giving and sharing with others is tremendously important and is one of the ways we reflect God's love, we should use the rewards of our labor or work to first ensure that our family needs are met. However, we must be careful not to become addicted to an ever-increasing lifestyle of comfort.

John Piper wrote, *"The issue is not how much a person makes. Big industry and big salaries are a fact of our times, and they are not necessarily evil. The evil is in being deceived into thinking a $100,000 salary must be accompanied by a $100,000 lifestyle. God has made us to be conduits of His grace. The danger is in thinking the conduit should be lined with gold. It shouldn't. Copper will do."* [4]

When you follow God principles for work, completing tasks with diligence and excellence, rewards are sure to follow. Be careful to avoid feeling guilty when you experience an increase in your income or assets. View this as God entrusting you with greater responsibility as His steward. Use your increase to give more glory to Him.

## Beware of the Bondage of Busyness

When we're stressed, it can be easy to sacrifice peace of mind in order to attain our financial goals. But this sacrifice is a form of bondage. In order to thrive in any economy, we cannot give up the peace that comes from walking in step with God's Spirit.

The bondage of busyness takes hold when we become so overwhelmed in any one area of life that our busyness disrupts our priorities as Christians. Often work is the biggest culprit.

A Christian's priority system should begin with an active, vibrant personal relationship with Jesus Christ. That means reading God's Word on a regular basis to understand His will for your life, and it means conversing with God in prayer.

Any Christian who is so busy that he has no time to study God's Word, pray, or serve other people is in bondage. When we become slaves to our busyness, we can easily neglect our families, which dishonors our commitments. We are responsible for the training of our children, and if we fail in raising our children according to God's Word, God is not pleased.

Being in balance with the world's system is risky, because the world has never been in balance with God's system. If you or your spouse are required to work 10, 12, or 14 hours a day to do a good job, make more money or just get ahead, watch out—that's bondage!

If you are in bondage, because of work or for any other reason, ask God to help you bring balance into your life today.

## Work in the Area Where God Has Given You Skill

One way to truly do well regardless of the economic climate is to work in an area where your natural gifts will allow for the greatest impact. It honors the Father when we are true to work according to our design. Ralph Mattson and Arthur Miller make this point quite well in their book, *Finding a Job You Can Love*:

> *"We please God when we act the way
> we are designed to act, when we are who
> God designed us to be. When such actions
> are carried out with the intention of being
> expressions of love to Him, they do in fact
> become expressions of love to Him."* [5]

A friend once helped me understand the importance of knowing God's unique design of my inner man. He encouraged me to seek understanding of my gifts, interests, skills and values and to operate accordingly in my chosen area of work. He said, "Chuck, a John Deere Tractor is not a Mercedes Benz and a Bulldog is not a Chihuahua, so you would not attempt to plow a field driving a Mercedes or train the Bulldog to sit in your lap. Likewise you should not work in an area where God has not designed you to be successful." How true.

Can you imagine a bluebird trying to be a woodpecker just so it can attract more attention? His bill is not equipped for drilling holes. A bluebird honors its Creator by being a very beautiful bluebird. Likewise, those who recognize their talents and use them for the glory of God become a magnificent testimony to the work of the Creator. And our work can and should be a means of offering ourselves to God.

Have you ever thought about your work being a means of offering yourself to God as a sacrifice? Think about that for a second. In the Old Testament, one of the big ideas behind the sacrificial system was that people were supposed to offer their first and best to God. God doesn't want leftovers; He wants first place in our lives. When it comes to work then, doesn't it make sense that we offer our first and best to God there? This means, of course, working hard and completing a task with excellence, but it also means being a good steward of our gifts, skills and abilities, so that we offer God the very finest we can. In other words, we need to discover how God has uniquely made us so that we can give back to Him the best of ourselves.

> **Have you ever thought about your work being a means of offering yourself to God as a sacrifice?**

Since our work is meant to reflect God's glory to a watching world, we need to recognize this as the proper motivation for our labors. Our work is a sacred act of worship. It is a daily opportunity to share God's goodness. If we are motivated by greed, pride or a desire to become powerful in the eyes of the world, we fail to achieve our life's purpose.

> *"So, whether you eat or drink, or whatever you do, do all to the glory of God"* (1 CORINTHIANS 10:31).

> *"For we are his workmanship, created in Christ Jesus for good works, which God prepared beforehand, that we should walk in them"* (EPHESIANS 2:10).

> *"And every craftsman in whom the LORD has put skill and intelligence to know how to do any work in the construction of the sanctuary shall work in accordance with all that the LORD has commanded"* (EXODUS 36:1).

thrive | **chapter 3**

# Get Free,
# Stay Free

*Amazing Grace* is a beautiful movie depicting the courageous battle that William Wilberforce waged to end the human slave trade in the British Empire. The story portrays John Newton, the former slave trader who penned the lyrics to the Christian hymn, tormented by memories of his role in the industry. Apart from the most extreme of circumstances, no one who understands the horrors of human slavery would willingly commit to being the bond-slave of another person, yet the Bible says that's what millions of people across the world do, simply by borrowing money. Granted, it is a lesser form of bondage, but the devastation caused by debt can be severe and has even led some to take their own lives.

A disciple of Jesus Christ should be free of all masters except Jesus, but debt makes a person a slave to the lender. Jesus Christ was a slave, but only to the will of His Father; he had no human masters. Likewise, we should be free to completely obey God's will at any time. After all, being able to live in such freedom is really what it means to thrive.

The amount of debt in our nation has exploded— government debt and personal debt. Just look around— we are drowning in a sea of debt. More than 1 million individuals file for bankruptcy every year.

Much financial tension results from believing the "gospel according to Madison Avenue," i.e., buy now and pay later with easy monthly payments. But nothing about those monthly payments is easy. Advertisers fail to tell us the whole truth. They leave out one little word: debt.

# What Is Debt?

The dictionary defines debt as "money that a person is obligated to pay to another." Debt includes bank loans, money borrowed from relatives, the home mortgage, past-due medical bills and money owed to credit card companies. Bills that come due, such as the monthly electric bill, are not considered debt if they are paid on time.

# What Debt Really Costs

We need to understand the real cost of debt. Assume you have $5,560 in credit card debt at an 18 percent interest rate. This would cost you $1,000 in interest annually.

Study the chart below (continued on the next page):

### 1. Amount of interest you paid

| Year 5 | Year 10 | Year 20 | Year 30 | Year 40 |
|--------|---------|---------|---------|---------|
| $5,000 | $10,000 | $20,000 | $30,000 | $40,000 |

### 2. What you would accumulate on $1,000 invested annually earning 5 percent

| Year 5 | Year 10 | Year 20 | Year 30 | Year 40 |
|--------|---------|---------|---------|---------|
| $5,802 | $13,207 | $34,719 | $69,761 | $126,840 |

### 3. How much the lender earns from your interest payment at 18 percent interest

| Year 5 | Year 10 | Year 20 | Year 30 | Year 40 |
|--------|---------|---------|---------|---------|
| $7,154 | $23,521 | $146,628 | $790,948 | $4,163,213 |

You can see what lenders have known for a long time: the incredible impact of compounding interest working for them. If they earn 18 percent, they will accumulate more than $4 million on your $1,000 a year for 40 years! Is there any wonder credit card companies are eager for you to become one of their borrowers? Now compare the $40,000 you paid in interest over 40 years with the $126,840 you would have accumulated if you earned just 5 percent on $1,000 each year.

Debt has a much higher cost than many realize. Stop to consider this: When you assume debt of $5,560 and pay $1,000 a year in interest versus earning a 5 percent return on that $1000, it actually costs you $166,840 over 40 years— that's $40,000 you would have paid in interest, plus $126,840 you missed out by not investing. The next time you are tempted to purchase something with debt, ask yourself if the long-term benefits of staying out of debt outweigh the short-term benefits of the purchase.

In addition to the financial cost, debt often increases stress, which contributes to mental, physical and emotional fatigue. It can stifle creativity and harm relationships. Many people raise their lifestyle through debt, only to discover that its burden then controls their lifestyle.

# The Bible on Debt

Scripture does not say that debt is a sin, but it discourages it. Remember, God loves us and has given us these principles for our benefit. Read the first portion of Romans 13:8 from several different translations: *"Owe no man any thing"* (KJV). *"Let no debt remain outstanding"* (NIV). *"Don't run up debts"* (MSG). *"Owe nothing to anyone"* (NASB). *"Keep out of debt and owe no man anything"* (AMP).

## 1. Debt is considered slavery.

Proverbs 22:7 reads: *"The rich rules over the poor, and the borrower is slave to the lender."* When we are in debt, we're a servant to the lender. And the deeper we are in debt, the more like servants we become. We don't have the freedom to decide where to spend our income because it is already obligated to meet these debts.

In 1 Corinthians 7:23, Paul writes, *"You were bought with a price; do not become slaves of men"* (NASB). Our Father made the ultimate sacrifice by giving His Son, the Lord Jesus Christ, to die for us. And He now wants His children free to serve Him rather than lenders.

## 2. Debt was considered a curse.

In the Old Testament, being out of debt was one of the promised rewards for obedience.

*"And if you faithfully obey the voice of the LORD your God, being careful to do all his commandments that I command you today, the LORD your God will set you high*

*above all the nations of the earth. And all these blessings shall come upon you and overtake you. . . . You shall lend to many nations, but you shall not borrow"* (DEUTERONOMY 28:1-2, 12).

However, debt was one of the curses for disobedience.

*"But if you will not obey the voice of the LORD your God or be careful to do all his commandments and his statutes that I command you today, then all these curses shall come upon you and overtake you. . . . The sojourner who is among you shall rise higher and higher above you, and you shall come down lower and lower. He shall lend to you, and you shall not lend to him. He shall be the head, and you shall be the tail"* (DEUTERONOMY 28:15, 43-44).

National indebtedness is front-page news these days. The effect it has on our economy is tremendous, with hundreds of billions of dollars per year going to interest payments alone. Our national debt grows each year, so unless something radical changes, this current course will become unsustainable in the not-too-distant future. And more disconcerting is the impact our debt has on our standing in the world. We have less influence overseas, and less political leverage as a result. Borrowing has cost us much more than money!

## 3. Debt presumes upon tomorrow.

When we get into debt, we assume that we will earn enough in the future to repay it. We plan for our jobs to continue or our investments to be profitable. The Bible cautions us against presumption: *"Come now, you who say, 'Today or tomorrow, we will go into such and such a town and spend a year there and trade and make a profit'—yet you do not know what tomorrow will bring. . . . Instead, you ought to say, 'If the Lord wills, we will live and do this or that'"* (JAMES 4:13-15).

What happens when we assume debt and presume upon tomorrow? Well, let's take another look at our nation's debt. As of the time of this writing, our country is $16 trillion in debt (with a $400 billion annual interest payment!), and our political representatives seem incapable of changing course. This debt will be left to our children and our children's children. No human being can look into the future and know whether these future generations will have the capacity to pay the debt we've accrued. We're strapping hundreds of millions of future Americans with a nearly unfathomable financial obligation! Our decisions today are changing the course of our nation's future whether we like it or not. And though the numbers might not be quite as large, this same principle is true of our personal economic futures as well. No wonder the Bible discourages debt!

## 4. Debt hinders our freedom to follow God's leading.

Ron Blue, an outstanding financial author, tells of a young man who wanted to go to seminary to become a missionary. The young man had no money and thought the only way he could afford seminary was to secure a student loan. However, this would have left him with $40,000 of debt by the time he graduated. He knew a missionary's salary would never be able to repay that much debt.

After a great deal of prayer, he decided to enroll without the aid of a loan, trusting God to meet his needs. He graduated without borrowing anything and grew in his appreciation for how God could provide for his needs. This was the most valuable lesson learned in seminary as he prepared for life on the mission field.

## Permissible Borrowing

The Bible does not give us a fixed list of scenarios in which we can owe money. In our opinion it is best to avoid all indebtedness if possible, though there are a few areas where debt may be permissible, such as for a home mortgage, or for your business or vocation. This "permissible debt" should meet three criteria.

- The item purchased is an asset with the potential to appreciate or produce an income.

- The value of an item exceeds the amount owed against it.

- The debt should not be so high that repayment puts undue strain on the budget.

Here's how a home mortgage might qualify. Houses meet the first requirement since under normal economic conditions they usually appreciate. You can meet the second requirement by investing a reasonable down payment so that you could expect to sell the home for at least enough to pay off the mortgage. The third requirement means buying an affordable house—one with a monthly payment that doesn't strain your budget under any circumstances.

If you take on some debt, we pray you will establish the goal of immediately eliminating it. Most people can become debt-free in seven years or less.

# How to Get Out of Debt

Consider these nine steps for getting out of debt. The steps are easy, but following them requires discipline. The goal is D-Day—Debtless Day—when you become absolutely free of debt.

**1. Pray and obey.**

In 2 Kings 4:1-7, we read about a widow who was threatened with losing her sons to her creditors. When she asked Elisha for help, he told her to borrow many empty jars from her neighbors. Then God multiplied her only possession—a small amount of oil—until all the jars were filled. She sold the oil and paid her debts to free her children. (And we assume she returned the borrowed jars!)

The same God who provided supernaturally for the widow is interested in freeing you from debt. The first step is to pray. Seek God's help and guidance in your journey toward Debtless Day. He may act immediately or slowly over time. In either case, prayer is essential.

As people begin to eliminate debt, I have seen the Lord bless their faithfulness countless times. Even if you can afford only a small monthly prepayment of your debt, please do it. God can multiply your efforts. As you pray, ask God to place others in your life who will gladly share their wisdom and experience to help you achieve your goals.

## 2. Sell what you are not using.

Evaluate your possessions to determine whether you should sell any of them to help you get out of debt more quickly. What about the clothes you no longer wear? That set of golf clubs gathering dust? Is there anything you can sell to help you get out of debt?

## 3. Decide which debts to pay off first by following the Plan to Thrive.

At Destination 2 on the Plan to Thrive (included at the end of this book), you'll focus on paying off your credit cards because they usually have the highest interest rate. At Destination 3, you will wipe out your consumer debt: car loans, student loans, home equity loans, medical debts, and so forth. And at Destination 5, you begin to accelerate the payment of your home mortgage.

Develop a spending plan. A spending plan gives you the freedom to spend money with a purpose or strategy. It simplifies daily decisions and ensures that your priorities will be met. The deeper in debt you are, the more restrictive your spending plan will need to be while you pay down debt.

Call Registry at DoNotCall.gov to stop telemarketers. To stop junk mail, call toll free 1-(888)-5-OPT-OUT. Everyone should do this!

When people use credit cards rather than cash, they spend about one-third more because it doesn't feel like real money; it's just plastic. As one shopper said to another, "I like credit cards lots more than money, because they go so much further!" Unfortunately, far too often this false belief keeps people trapped in debt for life.

If you don't pay the entire credit card balance at the end of each month, you may need to perform some plastic surgery—any good scissors will do!

**7. Be content with what you have.**

Advertisers use powerful methods to get us to buy. Frequently the message is intended to foster discontentment with what we have. Here's an example of this strategy at work:

Not too long ago, an American company opened a new plant in Central America because the labor was relatively inexpensive. Everything went well until the villagers received their first paycheck; afterward they did not return to work. Several days later, the manager went down to the village chief to determine the cause of this problem. The chief responded, "Why should we work? We already have everything we need." The plant stood idle for two months until someone came up with the idea of sending a mail-order catalog to every villager.

There has not been an employment problem since! Now, this is an extreme example and one that shouldn't be used to denigrate the godliness of work, but it makes the point.

Note these three realities of our consumer-driven economy.

- The more television you watch or Web-surfing you do, the more likely you will be to spend money.

- The more you look at catalogs and magazines, the more you spend.

- The more you shop, the more you spend.

**The more you trust God, the less you'll want to borrow.**

There is an interesting passage in 1 Timothy 6:5-6:

" . . . *Men of depraved mind and deprived of the truth . . . suppose that godliness is a means of gain. But godliness actually is a means of great gain when accompanied by contentment*" (NASB). When we are content with what we have and wait to buy until we can do it using cash—that is great gain.

Learn to trust God and you will experience self-control. That sounds like a paradox, but it's the key to getting out of debt and staying out of debt. The more you trust God, the less you'll want to borrow.

Another way to gain contentment and break the hold materialism has on your heart is through giving. The cure for wanting things is generosity. Begin giving 10 percent of your income to support God's work to demonstrate He is the highest priority in your life.

## 8. Consider a radical change in lifestyle.

A growing number of people have lowered their standard of living significantly to get out of debt more quickly. Some have downsized their homes, rented apartments or moved in with family members. Many have sold cars with large monthly payments and have bought inexpensive ones for cash. In short, they have temporarily sacrificed their standard of living so they could snowball their debt more quickly. This is one of those areas of life where less is more. Those who have downgraded their lifestyle to get out of debt often find they are happier and more content with less stuff.

## 9. Do not give up!

The last step may be the most difficult. On October 29, 1941, Winston Churchill, Prime Minister of England, gave a commencement address. World War II was devastating Europe, and England's fate was in doubt. Churchill stood and said, "Never give in. Never give in. Never, never, never, never—in nothing, great or small, large or petty— never give in except to convictions of honor and good sense."

Never give up in your effort to get out of debt. It may require hard work and sacrifice, but the freedom is worth the struggle. To accomplish this goal and remain debt free, you will need to live within your means by establishing a budget that works for you.

# Spend Money on Purpose

How would you rather spend a Saturday afternoon—a) frantically trying to scrape together enough money to make it to the end of the month without an overdraft of your checking account or missing a credit card payment, or b) creating a budget so that you will finally be able to spend money wisely, without guilt or the fear of never having enough?

Strangely, most people choose option a. They fail to see the benefits of spending a few hours each month getting a handle on where their money is going in order to avoid spending many more hours trying to figure out where it went! In order to truly navigate any financial current, you must have a budget or what I like to call a spending plan. While it's certainly true that a recession can wreak havoc on any spending plan, you must have one in the first place in order to make adjustments to it!

Few people think about the possibility of economic challenges in the future. The subject is unpleasant, and so we put off planning for it until it's too late. Most of us, by nature, are quite accomplished in the art of procrastination. We easily find time to do the things we enjoy, but avoid doing the hard things as masterfully as the Great Houdini escaped from his handcuffs and chains.

But every extreme challenge requires a plan, just as any grand project worth completing. For example, if you were going to build a house, you would need a set of blueprints—a house plan. This plan would tell you the size of the house, and how big each room would be. It would tell you where the windows would go and how high to make the ceilings. You would see where to put in the plumbing for the bathrooms and kitchen. Obviously, you need this plan to carry on with the building of your new home, and no amount of procrastination will make these plans magically appear. The same is true of our finances. In order to reach our goals, we simply cannot neglect developing a plan of action.

In the Bible, God gave His people a detailed plan for building the tabernacle, the ark, and the temple. God also gave detailed laws that the Israelites were to follow while living in the Promised Land. The Bible is full of examples of the importance of planning.

**Every extreme challenge requires a plan**

Proverbs 21:5 tells us that, *"The plans of the diligent lead surely to abundance, but everyone who is hasty comes only to poverty."* Luke 14:28-30 says, *"For which of you, desiring to build a tower, does not first sit down and count the cost, whether he has enough to complete it? Otherwise, when he has laid a foundation and is not able to finish, all who see it begin to mock him, saying, 'This man began to build and was not able to finish.'"*

If plans are so important, why do so many of us think we can manage our finances without one? In a recent survey of Crown.org visitors, we asked how many used a plan for managing their finances. Less than half of the respondents reported using a spending plan. Many people hear the word "budget" and respond negatively. They think of a budget as being restrictive, too limiting, and too legalistic. Yet, in truth, a budget can be very freeing; it can bring peace and break the bonds of being a slave to our money.

A budget is simply a plan—a plan for how to spend the money we have. As Christians, we recognize that everything we have is a gift from God. We are not the owners; we are simply the managers of what He has entrusted to us. Knowing this fact should give us a better perspective on handling money. A budget is a great way to make sure we are being faithful.

Without a spending plan, it is difficult to know where your money goes each month and whether you will have the necessary funds for the things you need. The "not knowing" can create feelings of anxiety and fear. Financial problems can cause stress in marriages and other relationships.

When you create a spending plan, you can have the peace of mind in knowing that your bills will be paid, that you have funds available for emergencies and what you are able to spend for the things you need and want.

The Lord blesses us with resources (or money) so that we can use it wisely to fulfill His purposes in our lives and further His kingdom. Without a plan for managing our finances, we may never reach our goals and experience true financial freedom.

Many people just shoot from the hip, hoping everything will turn out okay, because taking time to track the numbers doesn't seem very enjoyable. Many of us don't particularly enjoy brushing our teeth, either, but we've learned that the discipline beats the alternative—by a long shot.

**Not-so-good news:** Creating a spending plan will take some time and effort.

**Good news:** It will be customized to meet your needs.

**Better news:** It will save lots of time and effort in years to come.

**Best news:** It will pay off for the rest of your life.

Rather than being an inflexible straitjacket, a spending plan delivers surprising freedom. It removes mystery, fear and the exhaustion of struggling to keep our noses above the water line of debt.

## Steps to Create a Spending Plan

Creating a spending plan that fits you perfectly is the goal for this chapter. We'll follow several logical steps in the process.

### Step 1—List Monthly Household Expenditures.

The first step to creating a spending plan is to make a list of all of your monthly expenses. Start with the expenses that are fixed—payments that stay the same no matter what. Be sure to set aside your tithe on the front end and honor God with your first and best.

## a. **Fixed Expenses**

- Tithe
- Federal and State income taxes and Social Security taxes (if taxes are deducted, ignore this item)
- Housing expenses (payment/rent)
- Residence (Real Estate) taxes
- Home or Renter's insurance
- Other

**NOTE: In order to accurately determine variable expenses, both husband and wife should keep an expense diary for 30 days. Every expenditure, even small purchases, should be listed.**

Next, list your variable expenses—those obligations that are non-negotiable, but where the amount can fluctuate.

## b. **Variable Expenses**

- Food
- Outstanding debts
- Utilities
- Insurance (life, health, auto)
- Entertainment / recreation
- Clothing
- Medical / dental
- Savings / miscellaneous

NOTE: *In order to accurately determine variable expenses, both husband and wife should keep an expense diary for 30 days. Every expenditure, even small purchases, should be listed.*

### Step 2—List Available Monthly Income.

Make sure that you include all income sources, not just your regular salary. If your income varies from month to month, use a yearly average divided by 12 to establish a monthly average.

- Salary
- Rents
- Interest
- Dividends
- Income tax refund
- Notes (loans you have made to others that are now being repaid to you)
- Other

### Step 3—Compare Income Versus Expenses.

Here's where the rubber meets the road. Any effective spending plan will create margin so that your expenses (including amounts set aside for giving, saving and investing) can be covered by regular income.

We encourage couples to base their spending plan, as much as possible, on one spouse's income—thereby reducing the family's vulnerability to lost income due to

illness, pregnancy, or a change in employment.
The other spouse's income can be allocated to one-time purchases—vacations, furniture, cars—or to savings, debt reduction or giving.

If you are in the fortunate position of having total income that exceeds total expenses, your spending plan's primary job will be to speed your progress towards the ultimate goal of financial freedom—including the ability to serve in any way God directs without the need of a salary.

If, however, your expenses exceed income (or you simply desire more stringent controls in spending), you will need to analyze each spending plan category to reduce expenses. These categories are outlined below along with some guidance for the percentage of your income they will probably require.

The percentage of net income we suggest for each category is based on successful spending plans for families of four with a $45,000 annual income. These percentages are not absolutes and will vary with income and geographic location.

a. **Housing** (32 percent of net income)

Typically, this is one of the largest spending plan problems. Many families buy homes they can't afford. The decision to buy or rent should be based on needs and financial ability rather than on peer pressure or an unrealistic expectation of gain.

b. **Food** (13 percent of net income)

Many families buy too much food. Others buy too little. The average American family tends to buy the wrong type of food. The reduction of a family's food bill requires quantity and quality planning.

c. **Transportation** (13 percent of net income)

The advertising media refers to us as "consumers," but that's not always the best description. P.T. Barnum had a more apt word—"suckers." Often we are unwise in our decision making when it comes to machines—especially cars.

Many families will buy new cars they cannot afford and trade them in much sooner than necessary. Those who buy a new car, keeping it for less than four years and then trading it in for another new car, waste the maximum amount of money. Some people, such as salespeople who drive a great deal, need new cars frequently; most of us do not. We swap cars because we want to—not because we have to.

d. **Insurance** (5 percent of net income)

Few people understand insurance, resulting in poor decisions and lost money. Some buy high-cost insurance they don't need and can't afford; others have none, exposing themselves to unacceptable risk. It is important to know what kind and how much is needed.

Insurance should be used as supplementary provision for the family, not for profit. An insurance plan is not designed for saving money or for retirement. Ask anyone who assumed it was; the ultimate result was disillusionment.

One of your best insurance assets is to have a trustworthy agent who will create a simple plan to analyze your exact needs. Independent agents can select from several different companies to provide you with the best possible options.

e. **Debts** (5 percent of net income)

It would be great if most families had debt payments requiring no more than 5 percent of their budget. Unfortunately, the norm in American families far exceeds this amount because of the proliferation of credit cards, bank loans, and installment credit. What can you do once this situation exists?

- Destroy all credit cards as a first step

- Establish a payment schedule that includes all creditors

- Contact all creditors, honestly relate your problems, and arrange an equitable repayment plan

- Buy on a cash basis, and sacrifice your wants and desires until you are current

## f. **Entertainment/Recreation**
(5 percent of net income)

We are a recreation-oriented culture. That is not necessarily bad if put in the proper perspective. But those who are in debt cannot use their creditor's money to entertain themselves. The normal tendency is to escape pain for the moment—even if the problems then become more acute. We must resist this urge and control recreation and entertainment expenses while in debt.

What a terrible witness it is for a follower of Christ who is in financial bondage to indulge at the expense of others. God knows we need rest and relaxation; once our attitude is correct, He will often provide it from unexpected sources. Every believer, whether in debt or not, should seek to reduce entertainment expenses. This usually can be done without sacrificing quality family time.

## g. **Clothing** (5 percent of net income)

Many families in debt sacrifice this area in their budget because of excesses in other areas. Prudent planning and buying can clothe any family neatly without great expense.

- Save enough money to buy without using credit

- Educate family members on care of clothing

- Apply discipline with children to enforce these habits

- Develop skills in making and mending clothing

- Avoid the trap of fashion/fad consciousness—especially when it means buying expensive labels for no functional reason. When possible, buy clothes with a classic style that meet a need rather than clothes that make a temporary fashion statement.

# BUDGET HINTS

- Make a written list of clothing needs and purchase during the "off" season when possible
- Select outfits that can be mixed and used in multiple combinations rather than as a single set
- Shop at authentic factory outlet stores for close-out values of top quality
- Watch garage sales, consignment shops and thrift stores for outstanding values
- Select clothing made of home-washable fabrics
- Practice early repair for damaged clothing
- Learn to utilize all clothing fully (especially children's wear)
- Develop a network of families that exchange or hand down clothing without cost among the groups

h. **Savings** (5 percent of net income)

It is important to establish regular saving in your spending plan. Without a habit of saving, the use of credit and its resulting debt becomes a lifelong prison.

i. **Medical/Dental expenses**
   (6 percent of net income)

You must anticipate these expenses in your budget and set aside funds regularly; failure to do so will wreck your plans and lead to indebtedness. Do not sacrifice family health due to lack of planning; but at the same time, do not use doctors excessively. Proper prevention is much cheaper than correction. Many medical and dental bills can be avoided in this way.

Taking proper care of your body through diet, rest and exercise will usually reward you with good health. Abusing your body may not result in immediate consequences, but you will ultimately pay through illnesses and reduced abilities. This is not to say that all illnesses or problems are caused by neglect, but a great many are.

Don't hesitate to question doctors and dentists in advance about costs. Also, educate yourself enough to discern when you are getting good value for your money. Most ethical professionals will not take offense at your questions. If they do, it may be a hint to change providers. Shop around for prescriptions. You will be amazed at the wide variance in prices from one store to the next. Ask about generic drugs. These are usually much less expensive and are just as effective.

### j. **Miscellaneous and variable expenses**
   (6 percent of net income)

Some of these expenses occur monthly, and others occur on an as-needed basis (such as appliances).

One of the most important factors in home expenses is you. If you can perform routine maintenance and repair, considerable expenses can be avoided. If, on the other hand, you are just handy enough to turn a $50 repair into a $200 mess, you'll need to decide whether you have the

# SAVINGS HINTS

- Use a company payroll withdrawal, if possible. This removes the money before you receive it.

- Use an automatic bank withdrawal from your checking account into your savings account

- Write a check to your savings account just as if it were a creditor

- Begin saving at least a small monthly amount now. When you have paid off all consumer debts, allocate those monthly amounts to savings.

Many people rationalize not doing these things on the basis that their time is too valuable. Although this argument may have some merit for people who earn much more per hour than a repairman costs, unless they can earn it for as many hours as they want any time they want, it is probably a weak argument. And even for those who can earn around the clock, every hour of the day should not be tied up in the pursuit of wealth.

A part of care and maintenance around the home relates to family life, particularly the training of children. When they see Mom and Dad willing to do some physical labor to help around the home, they will learn good habits. But if you refuse to get involved, why should they? Where will they ever learn the skills of self-sufficiency?

Some men avoid working on home projects because they say they lack the necessary skills. Well, those skills are learned, not gifted. In addition to instructional videos that can be found on YouTube, there are many good books, often found in your local library, that detail every area of home maintenance. At some point in the future, many of these skills are likely to be necessities rather than choices.

### k. **Investments** (5 percent of net income)

Individuals and families with surplus income in their budgets will have the opportunity to invest for retirement or other long-term goals. This recommended percentage is a great starting amount, and then as debt-free status is achieved, more money can be diverted to this category.

l. **School/Child care** (5 percent of net income)

(If this category is used, other categories must be adjusted downward a total of 5 percent.)

A growing number of families choose private school and child care for their children. This category is for those expenses. Because this is an elective, it is not included within the normal 100 percent allotment, so other categories must be reduced to provide these funds.

m. **Unallocated Surplus Income**

Income from unallocated sources (garage sales, gifts) can be kept in the checking account and placed in this category. This category is also useful for recording income information for tax purposes.

## Variable Income Planning

Families with variable monthly incomes need a spending plan even more than families on fixed salaries. Many people with fluctuating incomes get trapped into debt because they spend what they make during high-income months and borrow during lean months rather than anticipating and saving for them.

Living on a fluctuating income can be very deceiving— and difficult. Months of high income can easily be construed as the new norm or a windfall profit to be spent on non-necessities. To properly manage variable income, conservatively estimate what your annual income is likely to be. Divide it by 12, and then use that amount as the monthly income for your plan. Put all your income into a savings account and withdraw your plan amount each month.

This method will allow surplus funds from higher-income months to accumulate in the savings account to provide the normal planned income during months of actual lower income. This is not hoarding; it is planning according to Proverbs 6:6-8.

## Pulling It All Together

Now that you have seen the general categories of expenses, one thing should be clear. Creating a spending plan is not mysterious magic. Nor is it too complicated. Although some people make a hobby of it and use sophisticated software that can generate a hundred different reports to give alternate views of the same information, others get by just fine with a fistful of hand-labeled envelopes.

**The basic steps are simple.**

1. Track all of your expenses for a month. Everything. (Include a monthly estimate for expenses you pay every three months or six months, etc.)

2. List your income for the month.

3. Compare the totals to determine whether you are spending more than you earn.

4. List your expenses in the category where they belong.

5. Check to see whether your category totals are within the suggested percentage of income.

6. Make any necessary adjustments (either to income or spending or both) to create a monthly surplus.

7. Spend according to plan, using discipline and patience to avoid violating your plan.

Remember that the race to accumulate usually ends at a different finish line than we expect. Effective advertising promises a finish line of wealth and happiness. Reality delivers a finish line of high stress, a crater of debt, and often the loss of the very things we worked so hard to get. Don't be the rabbit, getting caught up in the race.

Instead, be the tortoise, content to make slow, steady progress toward your goals. This is not difficult; it's just counter-cultural. And it's God's way. *"The plans of the diligent lead surely to abundance, but everyone who is hasty comes only to poverty"* (PROVERBS 21:5).

The Message says it this way: *"Careful planning puts you ahead in the long run; hurry and scurry puts you further behind."*

# HERE ARE SOME OF MY PERSONAL TIPS FOR LIVING ON LESS

1. Plant a garden and begin to grow some of your own food. Learn how to can the surplus. This is a great project to involve the kids in your new lifestyle.

2. Carry a small note pad or index card with you at all times. Write down every expenditure. Do this as a couple if you are married. At the end of the day/week/month, compile the expenditures in categoriesso you know where the money is going. Continue this habit until you have control of spontaneous, non-essential expenses.

3. Learn to wait 30 days before any major purchase and to shop for a bargain on every purchase.

4. Spend less on utilities: adjust the thermostat to be a little uncomfortable or turn it off and open the windows; take shorter showers; carry your garbage to the landfill instead of paying for a service.

5. Bundle your trips so that you drive less; shop for best prices on gasoline.

6. Join a food co-op or buy a warehouse membership; buy in bulk items you frequently use.

7. Learn to need less entertainment. Cable TV, Internet, movies, iTunes, sporting events and eating out are expensive forms of entertainment that can be eliminated and replaced with trips to the library, walks in the park or a picnic with friends as you develop an appreciation for less noise and more beauty

8. Buy used; shop at thrift stores and garage sales. Check for items on Craigslist and eBay from reputable sellers.

9. Learn to make things yourself that you once thought you had to purchase, such as clothes, gifts, cards, meals and treats.

10. Don't pay for services you can do yourself, such as taxes, maintenance, cleaning and home improvement projects. Check out "How To" manuals from the library and sign up for free classes to learn new skills at home improvement stores.

11. Think differently: Ask yourself, "How can I get this done for less? What would I do if I had no money to pay or this but still needed it? Who do I know that may have advice or resources to help me with this need? What can I exchange or barter to get what I need?"

12. Clear your mind: Walk more, ride a bike, cancel magazine subscriptions and stop watching television commercials that create a desire for more things.

# God's Provision Makes All the Difference

Years ago, God gave me an idea to develop a simple, step-by-step visual guide to help people understand the basics of managing money. We called it the *Crown Money Map*® and over 1,000,000 copies of the map are in use today all around the United States and in many other countries. The very first step on the *Money Map* is to create an emergency savings account by setting aside $1,000. Many Americans have money, but no margin. They live from paycheck to paycheck and would find it difficult to come up with $1,000 cash quickly in an emergency. So this is a very practical starting point. *But this is just the starting point.* The steps continue to the final destination, where he no longer carries any debt and is free to be more generous with their time and money.

We recently received a testimony from Joan, a woman who received her *Money Map* in 2007—just five years ago. She shared that at that time, she was in desperate financial straits. She thought the *Money Map* might give her some easy solutions for her money problems and relieve her stress. But when she opened the map and learned that she needed to save $1,000 as Step One, she began to cry out loud! This simple step seemed impossible to her at the time.

After Joan pulled herself together, she had a long talk with the Lord and asked for His help completing Step One. The rest of her testimony recounts how as a widow, she trusted God each and every day for the strength she needed to change the way she handled money. Five years later, Joan wrote to Crown to inform us she had completed Step One. She also mentioned completing Step Two, Step Three, Step Four, Step Five and Step Six and was celebrating paying off her final debt. With God's help, Joan is now totally debt free!

I like to say, "God is not a financial principle." His principles are given for our benefit, and they portray His beauty and character, but don't miss this point: God is God of the entire universe and nothing is impossible with Him. *Nothing.*

> *"'For I know the plans I have for you,"*
> *declares the LORD, 'plans to prosper you*
> *and not to harm you, plans to give you*
> *hope and a future'"* (JEREMIAH 29:11, NIV).

This verse should cause all of our hearts to leap with joy regardless of our current circumstances. It was delivered to God's people who were held captive in Babylon. They lived in something akin to a modern day refugee camp.

The Israelites had nothing when He spoke these comforting words to them. We take much hope and comfort from these words today, but we tend to skip over the Lord's instructions given just a few verses earlier. God had His part, but the Jews had theirs:

> *"Also, seek the peace and prosperity of*
> *the city to which I have carried you into*
> *exile. Pray to the LORD for it, because if*
> *it prospers, you too will prosper"*
> (JEREMIAH 29:7, NIV).

The Jews were to pray for and seek to help their enemies prosper, the very people who were holding them prisoner. In fact, the Lord said that their own prosperity depended on their willingness to help the Babylonians prosper! I call this the Principle of Reciprocal Prosperity. It is one of the most misunderstand financial truths in the Bible.

What are we to take from this? The Lord wanted to make Himself known to the Babylonians through funnels, not buckets. He had placed His people inside this foreign land to share His goodness.

Imagine if you are bucket. If left unchecked, our foolish pride asks (or demands) that God fill our bucket with money and possessions almost as a magical act that will occur without any responsibility or expectation on our part other than "sowing a seed of faith." This is the health and wealth or the "prosperity gospel," and it's an attempt to manipulate God to get what we want.

A more accurate understanding is that we are funnels and God wants to pour into those funnels so that we can bless others. God's message of prosperity in the Bible is that we are to be His conduits to help others prosper. That is, to discover the true riches in Christ.

If you are a businessperson, you will no doubt see the wisdom of the Principle of Reciprocal Prosperity. All successful businesses have a win-win attitude and strategy. If the company is able to serve others and meet the needs of the customer, the business will also grow and prosper. If it does not meet those needs, it will cease to exist. It's the very same principle here. An obedient follower of Christ is placed by God where the fruit of her life can be shared so others will have their needs met and the blessings of God will be spread. If we help others achieve their goals, we too will be able to achieve ours.

This is the aspect of serving others above ourselves that guides a good businessman
or woman.

## God's Part: Ownership

God owns all our possessions. *"To the LORD your God belong . . .the earth with all that is in it"* (DEUTERONOMY 10:14). *"The earth is the LORD's and the fullness thereof"* (PSALM 24:1).

Scripture even reveals specific items God owns. Leviticus 25:23 identifies Him as the owner of all the land: *"The land shall not be sold in perpetuity, for the land is mine."* Haggai 2:8 says that He owns the precious metals: *"'The silver is mine and the gold is mine,' declares the LORD of hosts."* And in Psalm 50 we are told that God owns the animals.

> *"For every beast of the forest is mine, the cattle on a thousand hills… and all that moves in the field is mine"* (PSALM 50:10-11).

**God created all things, and He never transferred the ownership of His creation to people.**

God created all things, and He never transferred the ownership of His creation to people. In Colossians 1:17 we are told that "in Him all things hold together." At this very moment the Lord holds everything together by His power. As we will see throughout this study, recognizing God's ownership is crucial in allowing Jesus Christ to become the Lord of our money and possessions.

## Our Ownership or His Lordship?

How we view God determines how we live. In the Bible God calls Himself by more than 250 names. The name that best describes God's part in the area of money is *Lord.*

After losing his children and all his possessions, Job continued to worship God because he knew His role as Lord of those possessions. Moses walked away from the treasures of Egypt, choosing instead to suffer with God's people because he accepted God's role as Lord of all.

If we are to be genuine followers of Christ, we must transfer ownership of our possessions to Him. *"So therefore, any one of you who does not renounce all that he has cannot be my disciple"* (LUKE 14:33). Sometimes He tests us by asking us to give up the very possessions that are most important to us.

The most vivid example of this in the Bible is when God instructed Abraham, *"Take now your son, your only son Isaac, whom you love . . . and offer him there as a burnt offering"* (GENESIS 22:2). When Abraham obeyed, demonstrating his willingness to give up his most valuable possession, God responded, *"Do not lay your hand on the boy . . . now I know that you fear God, seeing you have not withheld your son, your only son, from me"* (GENESIS 22:12).

**By Studying the Bible we can expand our vision of who God is.**

When we acknowledge God's ownership, every spending decision becomes a spiritual decision. No longer do we ask, "Lord, what do You want me to do with my money?" It becomes, "Lord, what do You want me to do with Your money?" When we have this attitude and handle His money according to His wishes, spending and saving decisions become as spiritual as giving decisions.

God's ownership also influences how we care for possessions. For example, because the Lord is the owner of our living space, we want to please Him by keeping His home or apartment cleaner and in better repair!

**Recognizing God's Ownership**

Our culture—the media, even the law—says that what you possess, you own.

Acknowledging God's ownership requires a transformation of the heart and mind, and this can be difficult. It is easy to believe intellectually that God owns all you have but still live as if this were not true.

Here are several practical suggestions to help us recognize God's ownership.

- For the next 30 days, meditate on 1 Chronicles 29:11-12 when you first awake and just before going to sleep.

- Be careful in the use of personal pronouns; consider substituting "the" or "the Lord's" for "my," "mine," and "ours."

- For the next 30 days, ask God to make you aware of His ownership.

- Establish the habit of acknowledging God's ownership every time you purchase an item.

Recognizing God's ownership is important in learning contentment. When you believe you own a particular possession, circumstances surrounding it will affect your attitude. If it's favorable, you will be happy, if it's a difficult circumstance, you will be discontent.

Shortly after Jim came to grips with God's ownership, he purchased a car. He had driven the car only two days before someone rammed into the side of it. Jim's first reaction was "Lord, I don't know why You want a dent in Your car, but now You've got a big one!" Jim was learning contentment!

## Control

Besides being Creator and Owner, God is ultimately in control of every event. *"We adore you as the one who is over all things"* (1 CHRONICLES 29:11, NLT). *"Whatever the*

LORD *pleases, he does, in heaven and in earth"* (PSALM 135:6). And in the book of Daniel, King Nebuchadnezzar stated: *"I praised the Most High; I honored and glorified Him who lives forever. . . . He does as He pleases with the powers of heaven and the peoples of the earth. No one can hold back His hand or say to him: 'What have you done?'"* (DANIEL 4:34-35, NIV).

God is also in control of difficult events. *"I am the LORD, and there is no other, the One forming light and creating darkness, causing well-being and creating calamity; I am the LORD who does all these"* (ISAIAH 45:6-7).

It is important for us to realize that our heavenly Father uses even seemingly devastating circumstances for ultimate good in the lives of the godly. *"And we know that for those who love God all things work together for good, for those who are called according to his purpose"* (ROMANS 8:28). The Lord allows difficult circumstances for three reasons.

## 1. He accomplishes His intentions.

This is illustrated in the life of Joseph, who was sold into slavery as a teenager by his jealous brothers. Joseph later said to his brothers: *"And do not be distressed or angry with yourselves because you sold me here, for God sent me before you to preserve life. . . . So it was not you who sent me here, but God. . . . You meant evil against me, but God intended it for good"* (GENESIS 45:5, 8; 50:20).

## 2. He develops our character.

Godly character, something that is precious in the sight of God, is often developed during trying times. *"We also rejoice in our sufferings, because we know that suffering produces perseverance; perseverance, character"* (ROMANS 5:3-4, NIV).

## 3. He disciplines His children.

*"Those whom the LORD loves He disciplines. . . . He disciplines us for our good, so that we may share His holiness. All discipline for the moment seems not to be joyful, but sorrowful; yet to those who have been trained by it, afterwards it yields the peaceful fruit of righteousness"* (HEBREWS 12:6, 10-11, NASB).

When we are disobedient, we can expect our loving Lord to discipline us, often through difficult circumstances. His purpose is to encourage us to trust Him more fully and "share His holiness." You can be at peace knowing that your loving heavenly Father is in control of every situation you will ever face. He will use every one of them for a good purpose.

## God is the Provider

The Lord promises to provide our needs. *"But seek first the kingdom of God and his righteousness, and all these things [food and clothing] will be added to you"* (MATTHEW 6:33).

The same Lord who fed manna to the children of Israel during their 40 years of wandering in the wilderness and who fed five thousand with only five loaves and two fish has promised to provide our needs. This is the same Lord who told Elijah, *"I have commanded the ravens feed you. . . . The ravens brought him bread and meat in the morning, and bread and meat in the evening"* (1 KINGS 17:4, 6).

God is both predictable and unpredictable. God is totally predictable in His faithfulness to provide for our needs. What we cannot predict is how He will provide. He uses different and often surprising means. He may provide an increase in income or a gift. And at times, He may provide an opportunity to stretch limited resources through money-saving purchases. Regardless of how He chooses to provide for our needs, God is completely reliable.

Charles Allen tells a story that illustrates this principle. As World War II was drawing to a close, the Allied armies gathered up many orphans and placed them in camps where they were well fed. But despite excellent care, the orphans were afraid and slept poorly.

Finally, a doctor came up with a solution. When the children were put to bed, he gave each of them a piece of bread to hold. Any hungry children could get more to eat, but when they were finished, they would still have this piece of bread just to hold—not to eat.

This piece of bread produced wonderful results. The children went to bed knowing instinctively they would have food to eat the next day. That guarantee gave them restful sleep.

Similarly, God has given us His guarantee—our "piece

of bread." As we cling to His promises of provision, we can relax and be content. *"And my God will supply every need of yours according to his riches . . ."* (PHILIPPIANS 4:19).

## Needs Vs. Wants

The Lord instructs us to be content when our basic needs are met. *"But if we have food and clothing, with these we will be content"* (1 TIMOTHY 6:8). It is important to understand the difference between a need and a want. Needs are the basic necessities of life—food, clothing, and shelter. Wants are anything in excess of needs. God may allow us to have our wants, but He has not promised to provide all of them.

|  | **Needs** | **Wants** | **Desires** |
|---|---|---|---|
| **Clothing:** | Discount Store or Used Clothing | Department Store | Designer Labels or Custom-Tailored |
| **Food:** | Tuna | Shrimp | Lobster |
| **Transportation:** | Used Car or Public Transportation | New or Used Luxury Car | New Luxury Vehicle |

## Getting to Know God

God, as He is revealed in Scripture, is much different than most people imagine. We tend to shrink Him down to our human abilities and limitations, forgetting that He *"stretched out the heavens and laid the foundations of the earth"* (ISAIAH 51:13). By studying the Bible and spending time talking with Him we can expand our vision

of who He is. The following are a just a few samples.
*He is Lord of the universe.*

Carefully review some of His names and attributes:
Creator, the Almighty, eternal, all-knowing, all-powerful,
awesome, Lord of lords, and King of kings. God's power
and ability are beyond our understanding.

Astronomers estimate that there are more than 100
billion galaxies in the universe, each containing billions
of stars. The distance from one end of a galaxy to the
other is often measured in millions of light years. Though
our sun is a relatively small star, it could contain more
than one million earths, and it has temperatures of 20
million degrees at its center. Isaiah wrote, *"Lift up your
eyes on high and see who has created these stars. . . . He
calls them all by name; because of the greatness of His
might and the strength of His power, not one of them is
missing"* (ISAIAH 40:26, NASB).

*He is Lord of the nations.*

God established the nations. Acts 17:26 says, *"And he
made from one man every nation of mankind to live on all
the face of the earth, having determined allotted periods
and the boundaries of their dwelling place."*

God is far above all national leaders and powers. Isaiah
40:21-23 tells us, *"Do you not know? Have you not heard?
. . . It is He who sits above the circle of the earth, and
its inhabitants are like grasshoppers . . . He it is who
reduces rulers to nothing, who makes the judges of the
earth meaningless"* (NASB). From Isaiah 40:15, 17 we read,

*"Behold, the nations are like a drop from a bucket, and are accounted as the dust on the scales . . . All the nations are as nothing before Him."*

### He is Lord of the individual.

Psalm 139:3-4, 16 reveals God's involvement with each of us as individuals. *"You are familiar with all my ways. Before a word is on my tongue you know it completely, O LORD. . . . All the days ordained for me were written in your book before one of them came to be"* (NIV). The Lord is so involved in our lives that He reassures us, "But even the hairs of your head are all numbered" (MATTHEW 10:30). Our heavenly Father is the One who knows us the best and loves us the most.

God hung the stars in space, fashioned the earth's towering mountains and mighty oceans, and determined the destiny of nations. Jeremiah observed: *"Nothing is too hard for You"* (JEREMIAH 32:17). Yet God knows when a sparrow falls to the ground. Nothing in this study is more important than catching the vision of who God is and what responsibilities He retains in our finances.

### Summary of God's Part

The Lord did not design people to shoulder the responsibilities that only He can carry. Jesus said, *"Come to Me, all who are weary and heavy-laden, and I will give you rest. Take My yoke upon you . . . For My yoke is easy, and My burden is light"* (MATTHEW 11:28-30, NASB). God has assumed the burdens of ownership, control, and provision. For this reason, living under His lordship is easy and we can rest and enjoy the peace of God.

For most of us, the primary problem is failing to consistently recognize God's part. Our culture believes that God plays no part in financial matters, and we have, in some measure, been influenced by that view. Another reason for this difficulty is that God has chosen to be invisible. Anything that is "out of sight" tends to become "out of mind." We get out of the habit of recognizing His ownership, control, and provision.

After learning God's part, you might wonder whether He's left any responsibilities for us. The Lord has given us great responsibility.

## Our Part

The word that best describes our part is steward. A steward is a manager of someone else's possessions. God has given us the authority to be stewards. *"You made him ruler over the works of your [the Lord's] hands; you put everything under his feet"* (PSALM 8:6, NIV).

Our responsibility is summed up in this verse: *"Moreover, it is required of stewards that one be found faithful"* (1 CORINTHIANS 4:2, NKJV). Before we can be faithful, we must know what we are required to do. Just as the purchaser of a complicated piece of machinery studies the manufacturer's manual to learn how to operate it, we need to examine God's financial principles found in the Bible to determine how He wants us to handle His possessions.

As we begin to study our responsibilities, it's important to remember that God loves and cares for us deeply. He is a God of mercy and grace. He has given us these principles because He wants the best for us. Most people discover areas in which they have not been faithful. Don't become discouraged. Simply seek to apply faithfully what you learn.

Now, let's examine two important elements of our responsibility.

## 1. Be faithful with what we are given.

We are to be faithful regardless of how much God entrusts to us. The parable of the talents (a talent was a sum of money) illustrates this. *"For it will be like a man going on a journey, who called his servants and entrusted to them his property. To one he gave five talents, to another two, to another one, to each according to his ability"* (MATTHEW 25:14-15).

> **God rewards faithfulness regardless of the amount over which we are responsible.**

When the owner returned, he held each one responsible for faithfully managing his possessions. The owner praised the faithful servant who received five talents: *"Well done, good and faithful servant. You have been faithful over a little; I will set you over much. Enter into the joy of your master"* (MATTHEW 25:21).

Interestingly, the servant who had been given two talents received the identical reward as the one who had been given five (see Matthew 25:23). God rewards faithfulness regardless of the amount over which we are responsible.

We are required to be faithful whether we are given much or little. As someone once said, "It's not what I would do if $1 million were my lot; it's what I am doing with the $10 I've got."

## 2. Be faithful in every area.

God wants us to be faithful in handling all of our money. Unfortunately, most Christians have been taught how to handle only 10 percent of their income God's way—the area of giving.

And although this area is crucial, so is the other 90 percent, which they frequently handle from the world's perspective. As a result of not being taught to handle money biblically, many Christians have wrong attitudes toward possessions. This often causes them to make poor financial decisions with painful consequences. Hosea 4:6 reads, *My people are destroyed for lack of knowledge.*

## Principles of Faithfulness

We can draw important principles of faithfulness from the Lord's parables.

## 1. If we waste possessions, God may remove us as stewards.

*"There was a rich man who had a manager, and charges were brought to him that this man was wasting his possessions. And he called him and said to him, 'What is this that I hear about you? Turn in the account of your management, for you can no longer be manager'"* (LUKE 16:1-2).

Two principles from this passage are applicable to us. First, when we waste our possessions it becomes public knowledge and creates a poor testimony. The steward was reported to him as squandering his possessions. Second, God may remove us as stewards if we squander what He has given to us.

I know of a businessman who earned a fortune in just three years and then went on a spending spree. Two years later he informed his office staff that he had little left and everyone would need to economize. Shortly thereafter, he left for an expensive vacation and had his office completely renovated at a cost of thousands of dollars. God soon removed this man from the privilege of being steward over much, and today he is on the verge of bankruptcy.

> Small things are small things, but faithfulness with a small thing is a big thing.

If you waste the possessions entrusted to you, you may not be given more.

## 2. We must be faithful in little things.

*"One who is faithful in a very little is also faithful in much, and one who is dishonest in a very little is also dishonest in much"* (LUKE 16:10).

How do you know if your son is going to take good care of his first car? Observe how he cared for his bicycle. How do you know if a salesperson will do a competent job of serving a large client? Evaluate how she serves a small client. If we have the character to be faithful with small things, God knows He can trust us with greater responsibilities.

Small things are small things, but faithfulness with a small thing is a big thing.

## 3. We must be faithful with another's possessions.

Faithfulness with another's possessions in some measure will determine how much you are given. *"And if you have not been faithful in that which is another's, who will give you that which is your own?"* (LUKE 16:12).

This is a principle that is often overlooked. One of the most faithful men I know rented a vehicle from a friend and damaged it in an accident. He told the owner what happened and then delivered the vehicle to the owner's mechanic with these instructions: "Make it better than it was before the accident, and I will be responsible for the bill." What an example!

When someone allows you to use something, are you careful to return it promptly and in good shape? Are you careless with your employer's office supplies? Do you waste electricity when you are staying in a hotel room? Some people have not been entrusted with more because they have been unfaithful with the possessions of others.

God promises to do His part in our finances; our part is to grow in faithfulness.

thrive | **chapter 6**

# Save a Portion of
# All Your Earnings

A few years ago, I was speaking at a local church, delivering a message similar to the one you're reading in this book. Afterwards, a woman came up to me and asked if she could tell me her story. She then told me, with tears of joy in her eyes, how she had recently replaced her home's water heater.

For many people, getting a new water heater is fairly mundane—but for this woman, the purchase represented something much more meaningful. She told me how, throughout her marriage, she and her husband had scraped by financially. They often had a difficult time making ends meet, and when something needed fixing or there was a small emergency, they'd borrow money—often from family and friends. But borrowing money never really helped. As soon as one debt was paid off, they would need to borrow to cover some other unexpected expense.

Now in her sixties, she told me how for years she been mortified having to ask loved ones for loans. The stress of living in debt and the accompanying embarrassment had taken a tremendous toll on her marriage, to the point where she and her husband had separated over finances.

But then she attended a Crown small group study at her church and learned biblical principles for handling money God's way. She discovered that by setting aside small amounts of money in an emergency savings account she could find freedom from the never-ending cycle of debt in which she and her husband had been living. Though it would be daunting to save the first $1000 for emergencies, the plan laid out in the small group study was also straightforward.

So armed with a plan of action and a new understanding of God's perspective for handling money, she reached out to her husband and the two agreed to work together, submitting their finances to the Lord.

Some time later, her home's water heater conked out for the last time. She began to cry as she wrote out the check to the plumber, but this time the tears were not from frustration (or because she had taken a cold shower that morning); they were caused by her newfound happiness! For the first time that she could remember, she had the cash to pay for one of life's interruptions— no stress, no embarrassment. But more important than any home appliance, by determining to handle money God's way, she and her husband were enjoying a renewed marriage—stronger and more joyful than ever before!

Can you see why we believe every family should allocate a percentage of its income to savings? Savings allows families to purchase with cash and shop for the best buys, irrespective of the store. And without savings, if there were an emergency (such as the one I just shared about the water heater) families would have to rely on credit and, ultimately, end up deeper in debt. Simply put, without emergency savings, borrowing would be a foregone conclusion. The use of credit would become a lifelong necessity, and debt would be a way of life.

Everyone in our society living above the poverty level probably has the capability to save money, yet many fail to do so because they believe the amount they can save is so small that it's meaningless. However, no amount is insignificant. Even $5 per month will add up.

Under normal conditions, we recommend that families work toward setting aside an amount equal to three to six months' salary for emergency savings, for those who have a steady income; for those who have a fluctuating or seasonal income, six months' salary is best. This type of savings is not long-range savings for college or retirement; it is non-allocated short-term savings designed to help compensate for unexpected emergencies.

## Extreme Saving Based on *The S.A.L.T. Plan*™

But that's under "normal" circumstances. Our nation's current economic outlook is anything but normal. I now recommend families allocate 20 percent of their income to savings until they have accrued 140 percent of their annual income. I realize that sounds like a lot of money, but extreme economic times call for extreme economic measures.

Where did 140 percent come from? The Bible. In *The S.A.L.T. Plan*™, I outlined what I believe to be God's saving strategy for extremely difficult times:

After several years of famine, Joseph had taken all of the grain and livestock from the people. When the famine persisted, he took the people themselves as slaves. Do you remember how he kept them from starving?

> *"Joseph said to the people, 'Now that I
> have bought you and your land today for
> Pharaoh, here is seed for you so you can
> plant the ground. But when the crop comes*

*in, give a fifth of it to Pharaoh. The other
four-fifths you may keep as seed for the
fields and as food for yourselves and your
households and your children.'"*
(GENESIS 47:23-24, NIV)

We see that this was the government, through a tax,
implementing a savings program for the people. Joseph
ensured that enough grain would be in the Pharaoh's
storehouses to feed the people when all other resources
failed them.

This is not the typical biblical approach to saving—that is,
waiting for the government to do it for you. In *The S.A.L.T.
Plan™*, you will do the saving. You will not wait for the
government to save for you. It is always God's will that you
rely on Him to provide through the resources He gives
you—not the government. There is another extremely
important lesson regarding saving that we can draw from
this example, and that relates to the amount of saving. In
Joseph's case, it was one-fifth, or 20 percent.

I do not believe God simply chose that amount arbitrarily.
I believe it is His intention that in times of extreme danger,
His people should set aside that proportion of their
income. This, then, is the savings goal of *The S.A.L.T.
Plan™* —20 percent of the income that God provides for
you. I know that sounds drastic, perhaps even desperate,
but I believe we must prepare for desperate times ahead.

### Saving or hoarding?

Unfortunately, in today's Christian society many teach that
to have a savings account is actually hoarding, because it

negates reliance upon God's provision.

However, this teaching is contrary to the Word of God as presented in the parable of the ant in Proverbs 6:6-8; *"Go to the ant, O sluggard, consider her ways and be wise. Without having any chief, officer, or ruler, she prepares her bread in summer and gathers her food in harvest."*

**The difference between saving and hoarding is attitude, not the amount of money.**

Within their colony, ants have calculated almost exactly what they will need to get through the winter. They gather and store that amount during the summer and autumn. Saving is looking forward to a future need and putting aside whatever is necessary to meet that future need so that borrowing will not be necessary. Hoarding is putting money aside for no particular reason, and that money will not be used even if it is needed.

The difference between saving and hoarding is attitude, not the amount of money. Saving is good stewardship, a hedge against future needs. Hoarding is a lack of trust.

Each family should set specific guidelines about how much they need to save. Then they must stick to those guidelines and not allow themselves to get caught up in the attitudes of the world.

God commands every believer, *"Do not be conformed to this world, but be transformed by the renewal of your mind"* (ROMANS 12:2). All believers should give evidence of their trust in God through the way they handle their resources.

*"Precious treasure and oil are in a wise man's dwelling but a foolish man devours it"* (PROVERBS 21:20). The common attitude presented in the Bible is to save on a regular basis, and it is important that Christians develop good habits to replace bad habits.

Every family should allocate something for savings. A savings account can provide funds for emergencies and is a key element in good planning and attaining financial freedom.

The practice of saving money varies widely by culture. I have been in African villages where saving money is nonexistent. Instead of money, these villagers view their relationships with family and neighbors as a form of savings and protection against future needs. While we might be tempted to judge them harshly for not saving, we are advised to respect the poor for being "rich in faith." Often, they have no other option but to trust God for their daily bread.

I have also taught in Asian cities where the average personal saving rate is 30 percent or more of annual income. People there have a high degree of discipline and control that enables them to store for the future. Often this drive is from what they describe as a "survival instinct."

Does the one culture practice wasteful spending and the other hoarding? We should be careful not to condemn or endorse either group without knowing their true motive for saving or not saving money.

Wasteful spending presumes that God will always provide for us even if we fail to do our part. Hoarding, on the other hand, presumes that we are "on our own" and that God will not keep His promise to provide for our needs. Both must be avoided.

We must have financial surplus to meet unplanned expenses and to share with others in need. However, it's also important to avoid growing dependent on money alone. Perceived financial "independence" can in reality be a hidden form of dependence, relying on money instead of God. Hebrews 13:5 should govern our attitude about financial surplus, regardless of the amount we save.

## Five goals you should have for your savings

Saving money with no plan or defined purpose is pointless because it will disappear every time the wind blows "unexpected" expenses your way. It's like running a race without knowing where the finish line is . . . you run but never get anywhere because you don't know what direction you're heading. Poor planning and lack of goals for your savings is the surest and quickest way to an empty bank account.

Here are five main goals you need to have for your savings. Read them carefully, write down goals that best fit your situation and begin putting the goals in place so you can finally build your savings!

## 1) Save money for non-monthly budget items

When doing a budget, it is vital to plan for expenses that don't occur every month, but do occur one or more times per year. Some of those expenses include:

Real estate/Property taxes
(if not escrowed)

Auto/Home/Life insurance premiums

Auto registration/tags

Christmas gifts

Home maintenance (furnace and air checks, etc.)

Kids' sports/School supplies/Tuition and other child-related expenses

Medical expenses

There are definitely others as well, but this will get you started on your own list. Make the list and start working it into your budget. Planning for these expenses by putting money aside in a savings account each month (and labeling that account for each category) will greatly reduce your stress level.

## 2) Save money for large purchases

Perhaps you will need to buy another vehicle sometime. What about a new couch, a new roof, a new furnace, and many other large ticket items—do you have money laying around for these items? Most likely not. If those expenses are coming, how are you going to pay for them? For most, debt is the answer: a car payment, a home equity loan, credit cards. I have a different, *completely crazy* idea: save up for the item and buy it with cash! I know this goes against the culture, but I promise you'll have less stress if you save for big-ticket items now and pay for them later with saved money.

### 3) Save money for an emergency fund

This is actually very similar to #2 above. If an emergency comes up, most people use debt to cover the costs because they have no money set aside for an emergency. By the way, a new vehicle or even a new roof is not an emergency. Those are things you know are coming, so you should plan for them. Getting laid off from your job is an emergency. That "plan" (or lack thereof) will lead a large amount of debt fast! Having an emergency fund of three to six months worth of expenses will prevent debt and help you sleep better at night.

### 4) Save money for retirement

I am not sure about you, but I don't plan on the government taking care of me when I retire. Therefore, I have to do something about it. I suggest saving 15 percent in a retirement account. For our purposes, I won't get into specifics about exactly where to put it. The key is to make it a habit to put aside a certain percentage for retirement investing so that you have money to live on and hopefully thrive on when you reach the golden years.

### 5) Save money for college

This only applies if you have kids, of course. College costs are extremely high and if you do have kids, it's a great idea to put aside money to help offset those costs. There are many other ways to go to college without debt, so this is not vital. I don't suggest saving for college unless you are fully saving for retirement, have a fully funded emergency fund, and have no debt (other than a mortgage). These goals are more important than saving for college, but if you can start putting aside even a little for college, it will definitely help.

thrive | **chapter 7**

# Never Compromise Your Integrity

The results of a recent global economic survey should not have surprised me. When asked to name the number one economic problem facing their nation, the majority of respondents selected "corruption." But that's not the surprising part. We all know that corruption is the number-one killer of an economy, personal or national.

**When asked, "Would you be willing to cheat or steal in order to meet your personal needs if you knew you would not be caught?" the majority of respondents answered "YES"**

Here's the answer that shocked me (and the researchers conducting the study): When asked, "Would you be willing to cheat or steal in order to meet your personal needs if you knew you would not be caught?" The majority of respondents—those very same ones who listed "corruption" as their country's number one problem—answered "yes"! They could see corruption as someone else's problem but were ready and willing to excuse their own lack of personal ethics.

Remember this key principle: Money flows towards trust just as water flows downhill. This principle is true for individuals, corporations and nations. It also helps illustrate why this is an important topic for each of us, and not just for someone we know.

Your integrity is priceless. It's interesting that integrity is highly prized in the world's view, as well as God's. In tough economic times, integrity is essential, since trust is the foundation of all financial interactions between people.

Integrity comes from the root word *integer*, meaning "whole" or "complete." A person with integrity is whole, complete, not made less by dishonesty. This is a true description of the person who is genuine or authentic.

The Bible summarizes the life of the kings of Israel and Judea with a single measurement. Either the king did what was right in the eyes of the Lord, or he did evil. The entire life's work of a king boiled down to that one measurement: integrity before God. In the same way, our lives will be measured by our integrity and any small deviation can destroy it.

During a talk I gave to about 200 business people in China, I was asked how the Christian businessman in Asia could operate in a system that was controlled by corrupt practices. White-collar fraud and bribery are rampant there, as is the case in many parts of the world.

I immediately thought of Joseph and Daniel who were both men of absolute integrity operating in hostile, corrupt nations. I replied, "If you are willing to pay the price of short-term losses, even if it means becoming the last honest man in China, you will eventually be recognized for your integrity. Even a corrupt ruler wants an honest man to run his affairs. Joseph went to prison and Daniel went to the lions' den for their integrity, but both were exalted to the highest levels of responsibility in their corrupt nations."

I then read from Isaiah 33:15-16:

> *"He who walks righteously and speaks uprightly, who despises the gain of oppressions, who shakes his hands, lest they hold a bribe, who stops his ears from hearing of bloodshed and shuts his eyes from looking on evil, he will dwell on the heights; his place of defense will be the fortresses of rocks; his bread will be given him; his water will be sure."*

The room was filled with spontaneous applause, not for my response, but for the wisdom and hope shared from God's Word.

God's promises to the righteous man are staggering, and His warnings to the evil are terrifying. To be truly rich, we must conduct every area of our lives with absolute integrity.

> *"The house of the righteous contains great treasure, but the income of the wicked brings them trouble"* (PROVERBS 15:6, NIV).

> *"Whoever is greedy for unjust gain troubles his own household, but he who hates bribes will live"* (PROVERBS 15:27).

# Financial honesty

A businessman once asked, "Do you think it's possible to be totally honest in our business society?" He went on to explain that he didn't purposely cheat anyone, but even when "negotiating" a sale the common practice was for the seller to begin at a price higher than desired, knowing that the buyer always started with a price lower than acceptable. His question must be a conscious thought on the hearts of many sincere Christians: "Can you truly be honest, and if so at what cost?"

## Money is an indicator

Remember what the Lord says in Luke 16:10:

*"One who is faithful in a very little is also faithful in much, and one who is dishonest in a very little is also dishonest in much."* The small thing to which the Lord is referring is money. Naturally, this also includes the pursuit of money. *"For where jealousy and selfish ambition exist, there will be disorder and every vile practice"* (JAMES 3:16). In Philippians 2:15, Paul tells us to hold ourselves above this wicked generation so that we can prove ourselves blameless. For this to happen, we must avoid the devices of the accuser and hold to the standards of the Lord.

## Why the dishonest prosper

There is little doubt that in the short run a deceitful person will seem to prosper. It doesn't take long, however, for others to recognize this attitude, so he or she must continually seek out new prospects. We must remember that Satan does have limited authority over this earth and can indeed provide riches. The problem with his supply is that it is always accompanied by fear, anxiety, anger, greed and resentment.

The biggest loss associated with following the worldly path is the loss of God's full blessings. God declares that if we do not respond correctly in such a trivial thing as money, we will not be entrusted with any greater possessions (LUKE 16:11).

## Material witness

Can Christians be honest in our society? They must be honest to experience the fullness of God's power and love. There will be times when it will seem that others take advantage of that honesty. The Lord knew that would happen. *"If anyone would come after me, let him deny himself and take up his cross daily and follow me"* (LUKE 9:23). There is often a price to be paid for following in the path of Christ, but there is also a great reward as a result of doing so.

## Honesty in Scripture

Hundreds of verses in the Bible communicate God's desire for us to be completely honest. For instance, Proverbs 20:23 says, *"God hates cheating in the marketplace"* (MSG). And Proverbs 12:22 states, *"Lying lips are an abomination to the  LORD."* And in Proverbs 6:16-17 we read, *"The LORD hates . . . a lying tongue."* Reflect on the following comparison between what the Scriptures teach and what our society practices concerning honesty.

# The God of Truth

Truthfulness is one of God's attributes. He is repeatedly identified as the God of truth. *"I am . . . the truth"* (JOHN 14:6). And He commands us to reflect His honest and holy character: *"But as he who called you is holy, you also be holy in all your conduct, since it is written, 'You shall be holy, for I am holy'"* (1 PETER 1:15-16).

In contrast to God's nature, John 8:44 describes the devil's character: "He [the devil] was a murderer from the beginning, and does not stand in the truth, because there is no truth in him. When he lies, he speaks out of his own character, for he is a liar and the father of lies." The Lord wants us to conform to His honest character rather than to the dishonest nature of the devil.

# Absolute honesty

God wants us to be completely honest for the following reasons:

**We cannot practice dishonesty and love God:**

Two of the Ten Commandments address honesty. *"You shall not steal. You shall not bear false witness against your neighbor"* (EXODUS 20:15-16). And Jesus told us, *"If you love me, you will keep My commandments"* (JOHN 14:15). We cannot disobey by practicing dishonesty and still love God. When being dishonest, we behave as if the living God doesn't even exist! We believe that He is unable to provide exactly what we need even though He has promised to do so (Matthew 6:33).

We take the situation into our own hands and do it our own dishonest way. We are also acting as if God is incapable of discovering our dishonesty and powerless to discipline us. If we really believe God will discipline us, we will not consider acting dishonestly.

Honest behavior is an issue of faith. An honest decision may look foolish in light of what we can see, but the godly person knows Jesus Christ is alive even though invisible. Every honest decision strengthens our faith and helps us grow into a closer relationship with Christ. When we choose to be dishonest, we are denying our Lord. It is impossible to love God with all of our heart, soul, and mind if, at the same time, we are dishonest and act as if He does not exist. Scripture declares that the dishonest actually hate God. *"Whoever walks in uprightness fears the LORD, but he who is devious in his ways despises him"* (Proverbs 14:2).

## We cannot practice dishonesty and love our neighbor:

God requires honesty because dishonest behavior also violates the second commandment, *"You shall love your neighbor as yourself"* (Mark 12:31). Romans 13:8-10 reads, *"When you love others, you complete what the law has been after all along. The law code . . . and any other 'don't' you can think of—finally adds up to this: Love other people as well as you do yourself"* (MSG).

When we act dishonestly, we are stealing from another person. We may rationalize that it's only a business or the government or an insurance company that is suffering loss. Yet, if we look at the bottom line, it is the business owners or fellow taxpayers or policyholders from whom we are stealing. It is just as if we took the money from their wallets. Dishonesty always injures people. The victim is always a person.

**Credibility for evangelism:**

Honesty enables us to demonstrate the reality of Jesus Christ to those who do not yet know Him. By remaining honest in our business and personal dealings, we send the world around us two very important messages.

First, we declare boldly that we can be trusted. If our word is true in our everyday interactions with people, we will have more authority as we share the good news of Jesus Christ with those around us. To most people, the messenger is just as important as the message. In fact, the reliability of the witness means everything.

Second, with our integrity, we show that our lives have changed. In our society, people who are consistently honest stand out. *"Therefore, having this ministry by the mercy of God, we do not lose heart. But we have renounced disgraceful, underhanded ways. We refuse to practice cunning or to tamper with God's word, but by the open statement of the truth we would commend ourselves to everyone's conscience in the sight of God"* (2 CORINTHIANS 4:1-2). Our scruples tell a story much more vividly than our words can. It's one thing to tell people how Jesus can change lives. It's quite another to show them.

**Even Small Acts of Dishonesty Are Harmful:**

God requires us to be completely honest because even the smallest act of dishonesty is sin and interrupts our fellowship with God. The smallest "white lie" hardens our hearts, making our consciences increasingly insensitive to sin and deafening our ears to God's voice. This single cancer cell of small dishonesty multiplies and spreads to greater dishonesty. *"One who is faithful in a very little is also faithful in much, and one who is dishonest in a very little is also dishonest in much"* (Luke 16:10).

An event in Abraham's life challenges us to be honest in small matters. The king of Sodom offered him all the goods he had recovered when he had rescued the people of Sodom. But Abraham responded, *"I have lifted my hand to the LORD, God Most High, Possessor of heaven and earth, that I would not take a thread or a sandal strap or anything that is yours"* (Genesis 14:22-23).

Just as Abraham was unwilling to take so much as a thread, we challenge you to make a similar commitment. Decide not to steal a stamp or a photocopy or a paper clip or a long-distance telephone call or a penny from your employer, the government, or anyone else. The people of God must be honest in even the smallest matters. Abraham knew that his first priority, above every other, was to trust God in obedience. His life and his legacy were dependent on God's provision.
Thousands of years later, our situation is no different. If we are to survive economic turmoil and thrive through the most difficult of times, we must be walking in a right relationship with the Lord. More than any savings goal

we might institute or plan for spending we could create, if we learn to rely on our great God, we will have taken the most important step toward achieving the only true security in the world.

thrive | **chapter 8**

# Take the Money Test

As I've urged you in previous chapters, one of your goals should be to save enough money to navigate a prolonged economic drought. By doing this, you will build up a substantial savings account, giving you a measure of financial margin. The purpose of this chapter is to help you avoid two potential dangers inherent in having this kind of money in the bank.

When difficult economic circumstances surprise you, how will you respond? Will you continue trusting in God and His goodness or will your heart turn to that high-balance bank account for security? Many people will say that they trust the Lord when times are manageable, but when the economic landscape changes, their honesty (or lack thereof) and their giving pattern show where they have placed their security.

## The Money Test

The Bible never condemns wealth; it only warns about the dangers of it becoming an idol and it denounces when money is gained through evil means or used for foolish purposes.

Like any organization, Crown Financial Ministries looks for honest men to serve in our missions around the world. It hasn't always been easy to find them. Eventually, our continent leader in Africa developed a method to determine who should join our organization. He calls it the "Money Test" and it works like this.

When someone expresses interest in joining Crown's mission, the leader arranges a phone call and asks the candidate to submit a budget for launching the ministry in the candidate's country.

After reviewing the budget, the leader will say that he wants to fly out to meet in person for an interview and that he is sending a few hundred dollars in advance for expenses. He asks the candidate to keep receipts for how the money is used.

Later, after the face-to-face interview is completed, the leader asks for the receipts. In almost every case, receipts are produced showing the money was spent on hotel rooms, meals and other expenses related to the visit. The interview concludes.

> He is only interested in one question: Did you use money for your own interests or His?

Unbeknownst to the candidate, the leader then stays an extra day in that country contacting hotels, restaurants and car rental companies to ask about their rates. All too often, the receipts indicate costs higher than the actual rates, indicating they've been falsified and the difference was pocketed by the prospective new hire.

Candidates who fail this small "Money Test" lose their opportunity for the far greater reward of a long-term job.

I believe God gives each one of us a "Money Test." He advances resources to us and will demand an accounting of how we spend the money. He is only interested in one question: Did you use money for your own interests or His?

*"One who is faithful in a very little is also
faithful in much, and one who is dishonest
in a very little is also dishonest in much"*
(LUKE 16:11).

To those who pass the "Money Test," the long-term
rewards are defined as the true riches. These are the
blessings of living according to God's financial principles
and enjoying both the present and eternal rewards for
faithfulness to Him. These are the riches that cannot
be lost, stolen or destroyed in contrast to mere worldly
wealth.

*"The blessing of the LORD makes rich, and
He adds no sorrow with it"* (PROVERBS 10:22).

## Blessed to Give

But beyond simple integrity, God calls us to be generous
with what's He's provided. In a sense, our generosity is
another kind of "Money Test."

God wants to spare us the sorrow that can accompany
worldly wealth. He does that by asking us to trust Him
enough to give part of it away. He wants us to let go of
it. In difficult economic times—even when we don't feel
so rich—it is important that we submit our finances to
God and act generously toward other people and His
kingdom. Otherwise, we may survive the economic storm
only to find that the financial security we so desperately
clung to never really had the power to rescue us in the
first place.

God took a risk to bless us so richly. The risk is that we might fall in love with the blessings and forget the One who blessed. To minimize that risk, God designed an economy quite apart from the world. It's based on sharing, not hoarding or squandering. It is vital that we learn to be generous with others to avoid the dangers of trusting in our possessions. As we advance God's kingdom through practical means, we experience true riches through giving.

We must stop putting our security in the abundance that God has given us.

> *"In all things I have shown you that by working hard in this way we must help the weak and remember the words of the Lord Jesus, how he himself said, 'It is more blessed to give than to receive'"* (ACTS 20:35).

> *"Honor the LORD with your wealth, and with the firstfruits of all you produce"* (PROVERBS 3:9).

## Tithing: Begging to Give

In the Bible, the eighth chapter of 2 Corinthians provides a powerful account of giving. Poverty was no stranger to the first century church at Macedonia, yet their generosity was so great that it continues to be a model for giving almost 2,000 years later. The source of their generosity could be found in their *spiritual* wealth, which overflowed in such abundant giving that the apostle Paul made note of it repeatedly in his epistles.

Paul says the Macedonians were pleased to give, and God loves a cheerful giver. *They gave of their own accord*, not grudgingly or under compulsion. They *begged* Paul for the opportunity to give, not having to be begged themselves. And they entreated Paul for the favor of helping support the saints. For them, giving was a privilege.

More than anything, however, giving seemed to be a natural response for the Macedonians. It was done in love as an overflow of the love they had received from God. It required no audience, and is followed by no reasoning or regrets. It springs from a deep spiritual relationship that puts God in the proper perspective: as owner of all things.

## Learning to Fear God

During Moses' time, the tithe was established so that the children of Israel might learn to fear God.

Deuteronomy 14:22-23 says, *"You shall tithe all the yield of your seed that comes from the field year by year. And before the LORD your God, in the place that he will choose, to make his name dwell there, you shall eat the tithe of your grain, of your wine, and of your oil, and the firstborn of your herd and flock, **that you may learn to fear the LORD your God always"*** (emphasis added).

But what about the implications of this statement today? Does it still apply to God's people? Psalm 111:10 says, *"The fear of the LORD is the beginning of wisdom."* If we want to be wise in handling our finances, we must seek wisdom from God. One of the ways God intends for us to do this is to acknowledge His Lordship by tithing to Him (giving Him 10 percent of our income).

When we don't fear God, we discount His Lordship and put our will ahead of His, losing our eternal perspective and allowing temporary worldly things to gain importance. We allow money and possessions to become our gods just as surely as the Israelites abandoned God to worship idols before the captivity.

The result for Israel was bondage in a foreign land. For us, it's bondage to stuff, which often leads to debt, stress, divorce and ruined lives. Striving after stuff also diverts us from the fulfillment of eternal accomplishment.

> *"For no one can lay a foundation other than that which is laid, which is Jesus Christ. Now if anyone builds on the foundation with gold, silver, precious stones, wood, hay, straw—each one's work will become manifest, for the Day will disclose it, because it will be revealed by fire, and the fire will test what sort of work each one has done. If the work that anyone has built on the foundation survives, he will receive a reward. If anyone's work is burned up, he will suffer loss, though he himself will be saved, but only as through fire"*
> (1 CORINTHIANS 3:11-15).

Imagine staring into eternity with nothing to show for our time here on earth. The length of this life and the things we substituted for God would be pathetically apparent.

Thankfully, life gives us a daily opportunity to make God our central desire and take steps to become generous givers.

## Is the Tithe a Limit?

One excuse for not tithing is that it limits the amount a follower of Christ gives to God. But 10 percent was never meant to be a limit. In fact, the Jews were admonished to give nearly one-fourth of their income each year.

With such giving today, the church could replace government welfare programs. But most people need a starting point. We can find no record of God ever asking less than a tenth from anyone. But if 10 percent seems like a tip rather than an expression of loving dependence, give 11 percent, 12 percent, or as much as you desire.

*Some have fulfilled their personal goals to give 90 percent!*

Think it's impossible to give like this? Remember, *"with God all things are possible"* (MATTHEW 19:26). Recently, I met a man at a Crown event who had made it his goal to give away $1 million over the course of his career. Now, this wouldn't be too impressive if he was a millionaire, but he wasn't. In fact, when he purposed in his heart to give this amount, he was only making $20,000 a year! Now, more than thirty years later, he's given above and beyond his $1 million goal and is still actively giving to the Lord's work. Nothing is impossible with God!

Living under God's lavish grace means we're compelled to give as an act of love and worship. God's desire is that we give with joy rather than out of obligation. *"Each one must give as he has decided in his heart, not reluctantly or under compulsion, for God loves a cheerful giver"* (2 CORINTHIANS 9:7).

Remember, the principle of God's ownership means that God doesn't own just 10 percent of our money, he owns one hundred percent. That's why we should never give any amount with the view that the remainder is ours.

# ANSWERS TO FREQUENTLY ASKED QUESTIONS ABOUT TITHING

**Q: When I calculate my tithe, should it be on my net or my gross income?**

**A:** Proverbs 3:9-10 says that God has asked for our firstfruits, which is the first and best of all that we receive. We interpret this to be our total personal income before taxes (gross).

**Q: Should I tithe if I am in debt?**

**A:** As already discussed, the tithe helps us learn to fear God, which is the beginning of wisdom. If there is anyone in the world who needs God's wisdom in the area of finances, it is a person who is already in debt.

**Q: Is it okay to take my tithe money and put it toward Bible college tuition?**

**A:** Malachi 3 says we are actually stealing from God if we don't pay an honest tithe. Saving for a Christian education is a good thing, but not if our lack of trust causes us to rob God for it.

**Q: Could tithe money be used to support secular organizations?**

**A:** The tithe is given in God's name and should be used specifically for His work.

**Q: Should I tithe from the profits of the sale of my house?**

**A:** I believe we should tithe on any profit from any sale, because it is, in fact, part of our firstfruits. Even if the profits are to be reinvested in a new home, a tithe should be given first. Remember, it was God who enabled us to realize the profit.

**Q: Should a person tithe on an inheritance?**

**A:** Yes. An inheritance is part of our "increase."

**Q: What about insurance payments received after the death of a spouse—should a person tithe on the lump sum or just on the interest earnings?**

**A:** Again, look at the principle of tithing on our

"increase." If insurance proceeds are paid in a lump sum distribution, a tithe should first be paid on the entire amount.

1. Afterward a tithe should be paid on any increase received (interest, dividends or growth) from the investment of those funds.

2. If rather than being paid in a lump sum, the proceeds are held in trust and distributed periodically, then a tithe should be paid on each distribution.

**Q: Wouldn't you be exempt from tithing if you were on a fixed income (Social Security, pension, annuity) and barely making ends meet?**

**A:** Money received from Social Security is a return of wages that were previously earned. For those who have tithed on their income during the period that Social Security was being withdrawn from their wages, it is not necessary to tithe again. However, remember that we are not attempting to fulfill a law when tithing, rather we are cheerfully giving out of a heart of gratitude no matter how God has provided for our needs.

**Giving Beyond the Tithe: Reasons for Giving**

Like tithing, giving beyond the tithe should be an outward material expression of a deeper spiritual commitment and an indication of a willing and obedient heart.

We should give as the Macedonians did, out of a grateful heart and with an attitude of joy. The cheerful giving principle of 2 Corinthians 9:7 applies to all giving, especially as increasingly large amounts of money are given.

Another reason for giving beyond the tithe is conviction. Perhaps the Holy Spirit is prompting you to give to a special cause. How can you determine if such a desire to give is actually from God or just an emotional response? Read God's Word and pray. If you are married, include your spouse in the decision to ensure balance in your giving.

Finally, some may have the spiritual gift of giving described by the apostle Paul in Romans 12:8: *"the one who contributes, in generosity."* These people live very disciplined lives, enabling them to give generously. They are especially sensitive to the needs of others and conscious of the need to check out every cause they give to. Generally, they are very prudent people.

## Giving Is for Everyone

For the majority of Christians, serving God will never lead to worldwide fame, writing best-selling books or singing before thousands of people. But regardless of the work to which we're called, there's hardly a follower of Christ who can't give; and when that giving is done in love, it exemplifies the greatest sacrifice ever made for humanity: the death of Jesus on the cross.

Jesus gave out of love when He laid aside His heavenly glory to come to earth. It was because of love that He became a servant and gave His life to save us from our sins. And the Bible tells us that God also was motivated by love when He gave His only Son.

Along this line, Dr. Charles Ryrie made a powerful statement about love and money that lays bare the truth of our devotion.

"How we use our money demonstrates the reality of our love for God," he said. "In some ways, it proves our love more conclusively than depth of knowledge, length of prayers, or prominence of service. These things can be feigned, but the use of our possessions shows us up for what we actually are." [6]

# Knowing & Doing

Zimbabwean President Mugabe attempted to lead his nation through economic reform by instituting a wealth redistribution plan. But because of the unjust and illegal means used to accomplish his reforms, economic growth in the private sector dropped off a cliff. This resulted in significantly lower tax revenues for the government. To make up the deficit, Mugabe's government resorted to additional borrowing, and ultimately to printing so much worthless currency that hyperinflation was estimated to be 6.5 sextillion percent at its peak in November, 2008. (That's 6,500,000,000,000,000,000,000%!)

A friend in Zimbabwe, a fifth-generation farmer who had been wealthy prior to the collapse, sold everything he owned. His land, farm equipment, houses, and cash-producing crops had been worth millions in US dollars, but his sale yielded him only enough to purchase a lunch without a soft drink! His life's work was stolen by the thief of inflation.

Brian Olderive is another friend from Zimbabwe. He lost everything he owned…not once, but twice! And neither loss was the result of personal foolishness or risky business endeavors. Similarly, John Enright, a friend from the Congo, lost all of his worldly possessions four times, each time while fleeing for his life during a prolonged civil war in that country. Yet all of these men are full of joy and have no lasting scars or damage from their experiences. In fact, they are some of the most mature spiritual leaders I have known. How can this be? Because they know and obey God's Word.

I think it's important to understand that economic storms sometimes bring periods of significant loss that are largely outside of our control. God's Word shows us how to do more than just endure the loss of money. His Word gives us instructions on how to manage it wisely and do well no matter what storm we are facing. It is good to know how to do this should it ever happen to you.

> "But recall the former days when, after you were enlightened, you endured a hard struggle with sufferings, sometimes being publicly exposed to reproach and affliction, and sometimes being partners with those so treated. For you had compassion on those in prison, and you joyfully accepted the plundering of your property, since you knew that you yourselves had a better possession and an abiding one. Therefore do not throw away your confidence, which has a great reward" (HEBREWS 10:32-35).

Obviously, these Christian friends I've described did not choose to lose their possessions; their money and belongings were taken from them. Yet they did not lose their joy. Why? Because they knew they had better and lasting possessions. They placed their confidence in the promises of God.

Historically, we know that when the economy defies logic it tends to right itself; when it is oversold, it tends to retreat; when it is undersold, it tends to advance. As such, and although I still believe that this economy cannot continue at its present rate without suffering irreversible damage, I am not suggesting that everyone run out and withdraw from the stock market or change all of their investments or retirement plans.

We may not be able to forecast economic storms before they're on the horizon. Further, we don't know what will happen or how best to protect our holdings when they do arrive, but God knows, and we can trust His guidance! That's why the Bible makes it clear that we must take God's principles to heart and put them into practice.

> **"If you know these things, blessed are you if you do them"**
> John 13:17

"If you know these things, blessed are you if you do them" (JOHN 13:17). Principles and best practices are of no value if we only know them intellectually. Knowing and doing is the key to experiencing the benefits of God's promises. Living accordingly will help you to thrive . . . in any economy!

thrive | **appendix**

# Your Plan to Thrive in ANY Economy

## Destination 1 – Make a Plan, Stop Accumulating Debt, Begin Emergency Savings

- Create a Budget—go to **planner.crown.org** to use our online budget tool
- Stop Accumulating Debt
- Save $1000
- Start giving regularly to the Lord

## Destination 2 – Begin Debt Payoff, Keep Saving

- Pay off credit cards using accelerated debt payoff approach, the debt snowball —**crown.org/Tools/Calculators**

- Increase savings to one month's living expenses

In order to get out of the unending cycle of debt, you have to keep saving. Divide your surplus in such a way that a percentage of it can go to debt payoff and a percentage to savings. Depending on your situation, it may be a 50/50 split or 75/25 split . . . as long as you continue the habit of saving while you tackle your credit card debt.

## Destination 3 – Eliminate Consumer Debt, Increase Savings

- Pay off all consumer debt (auto, furniture, student loans, etc. – everything except for mortgage)

- Increase savings to three months' living expenses
- Increase your giving to the Lord's work

## 4 – Save For Short and Long Term Needs

- Begin saving for major purchases (home, auto, education, etc.)
- Increase savings to six months' living expenses
- Adjust your budget to start saving 20 percent of your gross income, the amount recommended in *The S.A.L.T. Plan*™ (see page 82)

## 5 – Buy a Home, Begin Investing, Readjust Your Budget

- Buy affordable home or begin prepaying your home mortgage
- Begin investing wisely for the future
- Increase your giving to the Lord's work
- Begin saving for retirement—find articles and resources at crown.org/Library

## 6 – Eliminate Mortgage, Keep Saving, Create an Estate Plan

- Pay off your home's mortgage
- Complete The S.A.L.T. Plan™ saving goal of 140 percent of your gross income.
- Make sure your estate plan is in order

*Including Elements from the *Crown Money Map*™ and *The S.A.L.T. Plan*™

# Escaping the Auto Debt Trap

Car debt is one of the biggest obstacles for most people on their journey to true financial freedom because most people never get out of it. Just when they are ready to pay off a car, they trade it in and purchase a newer one with credit.

Unlike a home, which usually appreciates in value, the moment you drive a car off the lot it depreciates in value. It's worth less than you paid for it.

**Take these three steps to get out of auto debt:**

1. Decide to keep your car at least three years longer than your car loan and pay off your car loan.

2. After your last payment, keep making the payment, but pay it to yourself. Put it into an account that you will use to buy your next car.

3. When you are ready to replace your car, the cash you have saved plus your car's trade-in value should be sufficient to buy a car without credit. It may not be a new car, but a newer low-mileage used car without any debt is a better value anyway.

# Pay Your Home Mortgage off Early

If you own a home or plan to purchase one in the future, we want to encourage you to pay it off more rapidly than scheduled.

## Understanding the numbers

Every mortgage comes with a payment schedule based on the length of the loan and the interest rate. Knowing how this works will help you develop a plan for paying off the mortgage. Let's examine the payment schedule of a mortgage with a fixed interest rate, paid over 30 years.

The first year looks like this:

| Paymt. # | Month | Payment | Interest | Principal | Balance |
|----------|-------|---------|----------|-----------|---------|
| **PAYMENT SCHEDULE** | | | | | |
| 0 | | | | | $150,000.00 |
| 1 | Jan | $1,048.82 | $937.50 | $111.32 | $149,888.68 |
| 2 | Feb | $1,048.82 | $936.80 | $112.02 | $149,776.66 |
| 3 | Mar | $1,048.82 | $936.10 | $112.72 | $149,663.94 |
| 4 | Apr | $1,048.82 | $935.40 | $113.42 | $149,550.52 |
| 5 | May | $1,048.82 | $934.69 | $114.13 | $149,436.39 |
| 6 | Jun | $1,048.82 | $933.98 | $114.84 | $149,321.55 |
| 7 | Jul | $1,048.82 | $933.26 | $115.56 | $149,205.98 |
| 8 | Aug | $1,048.82 | $932.54 | $116.28 | $149,089.70 |
| 9 | Sep | $1,048.82 | $931.81 | $117.01 | $148,972.69 |
| 10 | Oct | $1,048.82 | $931.08 | $117.74 | $148,854.95 |
| 11 | Nov | $1,048.82 | $930.34 | $118.48 | $148,736.47 |
| 12 | Dec | $1,048.82 | $929.60 | $119.22 | $148,617.25 |
| **Totals for year:** | | **$12,585.84** | **$11,203.11** | **$1,382.73** | |

As you can see, the payments during the first year are largely interest. Of the $12,585.84 in payments, only $1,382.73 will go toward principal reduction. In fact, it will be 23 years before the principal and interest portions of the payment will equal each other!

Now here's something really important to remember. Interest is charged on the remaining unpaid principal balance. Look at the schedule above.

In January, if you paid your first monthly payment of $1,048.82 plus the next month's principal payment of $112.02, the principal balance would be $149,776.66. So in February when you make your regular payment of $1,048.82, it is applied as though it were payment #3. Now, look carefully at payment #2. You paid $112.02 extra and saved the $936.80 in interest you would have paid. That is a great deal! Can you see why I hope that you will catch the vision of paying off your home? There's nothing magical about what I'm suggesting. Once you understand how it works, the numbers will work for you.

### How to Pay Off the Mortgage More Quickly

There are several ways to accelerate the payment of your home mortgage.

### 1. Reduce the length of the mortgage.

If you need a new mortgage or the conditions are favorable for you to refinance, consider a shorter-term mortgage. If you can afford higher payments, go with a 15-year instead of a 30-year mortgage. The interest rate on a 15-year mortgage is normally lower than the 30-year rate, and the outstanding balance shrinks much faster. Let's compare a $150,000, 30-year mortgage at 5.5 percent and a 15-year mortgage at 5 percent.

|  | 15 Year | 30 Year |
|---|---|---|
| Payment: | $1,186.19 | $851.68 |
| Interest: | $63,514.28 | $156,606.06 |

If you can shrink the duration of your mortgage in half, the savings in interest is huge!

## 2. Add something to the required payment.

You can still accelerate the repayment of your mortgage simply by paying an extra amount each month or as frequently as possible. Start small. Each month put a little more on the mortgage to reduce the principal more quickly. The longer you do it, the more exciting it will become.

## 3. Bonuses and tax returns.

Finally, when you receive a work bonus or an income tax refund, give generously to God and then consider applying the rest to your home mortgage. Doing that each time it occurs can have a significant impact on paying off your home.

**There are three primary arguments against prepaying a mortgage:**

1. Why pay off a low-interest home mortgage when you can earn more elsewhere?
2. With inflation, your later payments are made with less valuable dollars.

3. You lose a tax shelter because the interest paid on a home mortgage is tax deductible.

Rather than take the time to address these arguments, we should recognize that the tax system in America is designed to reward indebtedness. We get a tax break for interest paid on our home mortgage. However, the Bible discourages debt. We simply challenge you to seek Christ with an open heart to learn what He wants you to do.

Let me ask you a question: How would it feel to have no debt and no payments of any kind including your home mortgage? We can tell you from experience, it feels great!

If you want to pay off your mortgage, it is a good idea to inform your lender of your plans, to ensure proper crediting of your prepayment.

# Is Bankruptcy Permissable?

A court can declare people bankrupt and unable to pay their debts. Depending on the type of bankruptcy, the court will either allow them to develop a plan to repay their creditors or it will distribute their property among the creditors as payment.

Should a godly person declare bankruptcy? Generally, no. Psalm 37:21 tells us, *"The wicked borrows, but does not pay back."*

However, in our opinion, bankruptcy is permissible under three circumstances:

- A creditor forces a person into bankruptcy.

- The borrower experiences such extreme financial difficulties that there is no other option. Declaring bankruptcy should only be considered after all other options have been explored.

- The emotional health of the borrower is at stake. If the debtor's emotional health is at stake because of inability to cope with the pressure of aggressive creditors, bankruptcy can be an option.

Declaring bankruptcy should not be a cavalier decision, because it remains on a credit report for 10 years, and it often impairs ones ability to obtain future credit at reasonable interest rates. Potential employers and landlords are also likely to learn of a past bankruptcy. It can haunt people for some time, and although it provides relief, it is not exactly the fresh start that some advertise.

If bankruptcy protection is sought, the Bible instructs us to continue to make every effort to repay the lender.

[1] Larry DeKoster, *Work: The Meaning of Your Life: A Christian Perspective*, 2nd ed. (Grand Rapids, Mich.: Christian's Library Press, 2010), 1.

[2] Op. cit., Chuck Colson, quoted in DeKoster.

[3] Ibid, vi.

[4] John Piper, *Desiring God: 25th Anniversary Reference Edition* (Colorado Springs, Co.: Multnomah Press, 2011), 203.

[5] Ralph Mattson and Arthur Miller, *Finding a Job You Can Love* (Nashville, Tenn.: Thomas Nelson, 1982), 38.

[6] Charles Caldwell Ryrie, *Balancing the Christian Life* (Chicago, Ill.: Moody Publishers, 1969), 84.